The Education Center®

Back-to-School

Grades 2–3

THE BEST OF **The MAILBOX®** Magazine

Great back-to-school ideas, activities, and reproducibles from the 1998 to 2002 issues of *The Mailbox®* magazine!

- **Getting Acquainted**
- **Organizational Tips**
- **Open House**
- **Birthdays and Celebrations**

- **Classroom Displays**
- **Parent Communication**
- **Classroom Management**
- **Art Activities**

And much, much more!

Managing Editors: Cayce Guiliano, Susan Walker

Editorial Team: Becky S. Andrews, Kimberley Bruck, Karen P. Shelton, Diane Badden, Thad H. McLaurin, Debra Liverman, Deborah G. Swider, Karen A. Brudnak, Sarah Hamblet, Hope Rodgers, Dorothy C. McKinney

Production Team: Lisa K. Pitts, Pam Crane, Rebecca Saunders, Jennifer Tipton Cappoen, Chris Curry, Sarah Foreman, Theresa Lewis Goode, Ivy L. Koonce, Clint Moore, Greg D. Rieves, Barry Slate, Donna K. Teal, Tazmen Carlisle, Amy Kirtley-Hill, Kristy Parton, Debbie Shoffner, Cathy Edwards Simrell, Lynette Dickerson, Mark Rainey

www.themailbox.com

Table of Contents

©2005 The Mailbox®
All rights reserved.
ISBN10 #1-56234-622-9 • ISBN13 #978-156234-622-5

Manufactured in the United States
10 9 8 7 6 5 4 3

Student Information Cards

Send your new students' self-esteem soaring when you greet each child by name on the first day of school! To prepare, personalize an index card for each child and glue on his card a photocopy of the most recent school picture he has on file. On the back of his card, list his date of birth, a home and/or work number where a parent can be reached, known allergies, and so on. Hole-punch the cards and secure them on a loose-leaf ring. Then use the cards to learn the names and faces of your new group of youngsters. During the school year, leave the cards for substitute teachers, carry them on field trips, and share them with classroom volunteers. You'll find that these cards continue to be an invaluable resource long after the first day is over.

Landria Williamson
Copperfield Elementary
Taylor, TX

Colorful Nametags

Brighten up your class with these easy-to-make name-tags. For each student, round one end of a 6" x 18" colored construction paper rectangle to resemble a crayon tip. Use a black marker to personalize and decorate the nametag. Then laminate the tag for durability and tape it to the student's desktop. What a vivid way to deck out desks!

Gina Parisi—Grs. 1–6 Basic Skills
Brookdale School
Bloomfield, NJ

Customized Business Cards

To make it easy for parents to contact you, use a computer to customize a business card especially for their use. Include your name, the name and phone number of your school, and an email address and/or voice mail number where messages can be left. Print the information on blank business cards purchased from a local office supply store. To create magnetic cards, attach the cards to precut business card magnets (also available from office supply stores). It's an inexpensive way to encourage parents to stay in touch!

Melrose Park School
Ms. Michelle Lechel
Room 10
School: 555-0114
Voice mail: 555-0179

Please feel free to call me with any questions or concerns that you may have regarding your child's education.

Michelle Lechel—Gr. 2
Melrose Park School
Melrose Park, IL

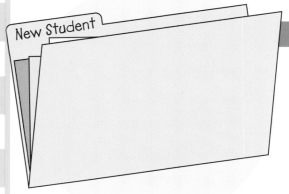

Future Enrollees

As you organize and update your back-to-school paperwork, go ahead and prepare for students who will enroll later in the year. Label a folder "New Student" and place inside one copy of each piece of paperwork you send home at the start of the year. When your file is complete, make several copies of each page and then assemble the copies into new student packets. When a new enrollee arrives, you'll be ready with a packet of new student information!

Patricia Wood
Valley Christian School
Northampton, MA

New Student Strategy

As you ready your classroom for the start of school, prepare for new student arrivals later in the year. Label each of several gallon-size plastic bags "New Student." Every time you label an item for individual students (such as a nametag, a lunch count stick, a cutout for the helper display, and a work folder), place an unlabeled item in each plastic bag. When a new student arrives, a smooth transition into her new classroom is in the bag!

Lu Brunnemer
Eagle Creek Elementary
Indianapolis, IN

New Student Checklist

☐ **Notes to send home**

☐ **Staff to notify**

☐ **Nametags**

New Student Plan

Prepare for new student arrivals with a handy checklist! To make a checklist of things to remember for new students, list the information by categories. Possible categories include notes to send home, staff to notify, and items to personalize, such as desk nametags. When a new student arrives later in the year, use a copy of the checklist to ensure that no details are overlooked. A smooth transition is bound to be the result!

Lu Brunnemer

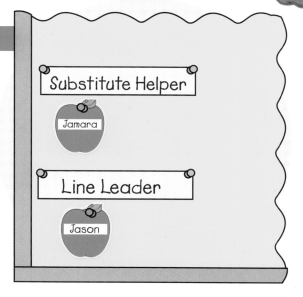

Substitute Student Helper

This year be prepared when a student helper is absent. Before school begins, add the job "Substitute Helper" to your display of regular classroom jobs. Each time you assign jobs, designate one child as the substitute helper. When a regular helper is absent, the substitute steps in and helps out. Rotate the substitute helper throughout the year so that all students have a chance to sub. This solution is sure to please your youngsters.

Betsy Strohsahl
Durham Elementary
Durham, NY

Lesson Plan Updates

Updating and reprogramming your weekly lesson plans is a snap with this slick approach! Create a weekly lesson plan format that suits your needs, and program it with times and classes that remain constant throughout the school year. Laminate the lesson plan and post it in an easily accessible location. Each week write in your plans with a wipe-off marker. As adjustments are needed or lessons are completed, wipe off and reprogram the weekly plan. Just think of the time you'll save this spring!

Stephanie Crawford—Gr. 2
Monticello Elementary
Tracy, CA

Picture Perfect

Labeling classroom learning centers is easy with the help of inexpensive, clear acrylic picture frames. Write the title and directions for each learning activity on an index card; then slip each card into a different frame. Place the frames at the corresponding learning centers. When it's time to change an activity, simply slide the card out of the frame and replace it with a new set of directions. Your centers will be neat and organized, and students will easily see the directions for each activity.

Liz Kramer—Gr. 2
Boyden School
Walpole, MA

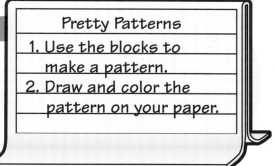

You are invited to an **Idea Shower**

Reaching Out

If you're a brand-new teacher or new to your grade level, consider hosting an idea shower! Send shower invitations to teachers who teach in your district and at your grade level. Invite them to your home for dinner or party refreshments, and ask that each guest bring a successful classroom management tip, a favorite teaching idea, or anything a new teacher such as yourself could benefit from. Your hospitality and your eagerness to learn from your colleagues are sure to be well received!

Susan G. Pelchat—Gr. 2
Forbes School
Torrington, CT

Supply List Tip

Consider this colorful suggestion when you update your school supply list for the year. In addition to your regular crayon request, ask each child to also bring to school a pack of eight basic colors. Label each child's eight-crayon pack with her name and then collect the personalized packs and store them for later use. You'll be ready with replacements when these popular crayon colors are depleted from a student's crayon supply. This approach is also a good deal for parents who can purchase the crayons during back-to-school sales.

Cynthia Ruth
Adair-Casey Elementary
Adair, IA

CRAYONS
Jamar
Kayla
Mitch
Sara

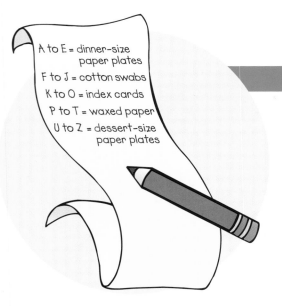

A to E = dinner-size paper plates
F to J = cotton swabs
K to O = index cards
P to T = waxed paper
U to Z = dessert-size paper plates

Gathering Extra Supplies

Here's another great supply list tip! Include on your school supply list an invitation for parents to contribute consumable supplies such as paper plates, index cards, and resealable plastic bags. To acquire an assortment of supplies, provide an alphabet code like the one shown and invite each parent to contribute the supply that's listed by the first letter of her child's last name. Acknowledge each donation with a note of thanks!

Jeanine Peterson—Gr. 2
Bainbridge Elementary
Bainbridge, IN

Lunch Ticket Butterflies

Make a class supply of these fancy fliers, and you'll have fewer lost or misplaced lunch tickets! To make the lunch ticket holder shown, pinch together the middle of a four-inch circle of scrap fabric, clip a wooden clothespin around the gathered material, glue the fabric in place, and attach a strip of magnetic tape to the back of the project. Attach a lunch ticket butterfly to each student desk. Or personalize one for each child and then display the bunch on another magnetic surface. On the first day of school, explain the purpose of the butterflies and make sure each child understands that he must personalize each lunch ticket he clips in his holder. One thing is certain—you'll have fewer students fluttering around looking for lost lunch tickets!

Susan Ream—Gr. 2
Artman Elementary
Hermitage, PA

Lost Tooth Certificates

Be prepared to share in the excitement when a child loses a tooth! Before school starts purchase a supply of small resealable bags from a craft store. Then use your computer to design a page of colorful certificates, making sure each certificate fits inside a bag you purchased. Print several copies of the page and cut out the individual certificates. Keep the certificates and bags handy. When a student loses a tooth, write his name and the date on a certificate. Then seal the certificate and his tooth inside a bag for a safe journey home.

Deborah Bellinger
White Oak Primary
White Oak, TX

Tooth Taxi

To guarantee that a lost tooth arrives home from school safely, provide a Tooth Taxi for its transportation. Cut out a small picture of a tooth and label it "Tooth Taxi." Secure the picture to an empty film container with clear packaging tape. When a student loses a tooth, simply drop the tooth into the container and snap on the cap. The tooth will travel in style!

Dee Kaltenbach Riesen
Tri County Elementary School
DeWitt, NE

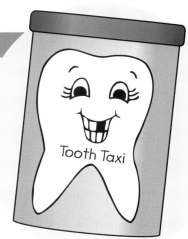

Pencil Pockets

These kid-appealing pencil holders are a teacher's dream come true! Collect pairs of outgrown or worn-out denim jeans. Cut out the back pockets along with the fabric to which the pockets are attached. Use a hot glue gun, Velcro fasteners, or double-sided tape to secure a pocket to each child's desktop. (If your pocket supply is limited, only attach pockets to learning center tables, reading tables, and so on.) There you have it! Pencil holders that are durable, quiet, and impossible to lose!

Jeanne Brown—Gr. 3
Rochester Hills Christian School
Rochester Hills, MI

Desktag Tip

Save time and money by laminating back-to-school desktags and using a wipe-off marker to program them. You can have desktags in place when the students arrive, yet you have the flexibility to reprogram them with preferred nicknames. And if a student is a no-show, you can reprogram her desktag for a student who just registered that morning. Then either permanently program the desktags that afternoon or cover the wipe-off programming with lengths of clear book tape (allowing you to later remove the tape, wipe away the programming, and reuse the tags).

Luella Brunnemer
Eagle Creek Elementary
Indianapolis, IN

Double Desktags

Two desktags are better than one, and here's why! Sometimes it's difficult to clearly view a desktop tag from a distance. So by placing a second tag on the side or front of a desk, classroom visitors can read student names more easily. In addition, if the second desktag is backed with magnetic tape and you have a magnetic chalkboard, students can use these tags for class graphs, class lists, and so on. Better make a second set of desktags on the double!

Candi Barwinski—Gr. 2
Fleetwood Elementary School
Fleetwood, PA

Student Mail Center

Having a mail center in your classroom makes it unbelievably easy to distribute paperwork for students to take home! To make a mail center, ask a local ice-cream parlor to save empty three-gallon tubs for you. (Half-gallon juice cartons can also be used.) Wash and dry each container and, if desired, wrap it in colorful paper. Then securely hot-glue the containers together, building a multilevel framework. Display the resulting structure in a location that is easily accessible to students. Personalize a small name card for each child and then use tape to suspend each card from the inside top of a different compartment. For easy distribution of students' papers, label the compartments in alphabetical order by first names. The mail center is now open!

Ruth Heller—Gr. 3
PS 156
Laurelton, NY

Pins for Pennies

Here's a quick and inexpensive way to create appealing pins for student wear. To make a class set of back-to-school pins, adhere on poster board one back-to-school sticker for each student. Then laminate the poster board or cover it with clear Con-Tact covering. Cut out the stickers and use craft or hot glue to attach a pin fastener to the back of each one. The unique welcome-to-school jewelry will make quite a fashion statement! Plan to create additional sticker pins to recognize student achievements, stimulate interest in topics of study, and celebrate student birthdays.

Ann Marie Stephens
George C. Round Elementary School
Manassas, VA

What a Year!

A few minutes each day is all it takes to create this school-year keepsake! Label a three-ring notebook, as shown, and fill it with paper. Near the end of each school day, review the day's events with students. Have a volunteer summarize chosen events in the notebook and then date the entry. Read the notebook to the class in May or June for a memorable look back. Wow! A lot happens in a year!

Melissa Gierach—Gr. 2
Dillard Street Elementary School
Winter Garden, FL

Introducing the Pack!

John   Maya   Seth   8 CRAYONS   Karen   Mitch   Rich

Jessie   Tonya   Lorie   Holly   Davis   Annie

Introduce your new pack of students with this colorful display! Personalize a crayon pattern (page 17) for each student. A child colors her pattern and cuts it out. Then she renders a self-portrait on 9" x 12" art paper. Showcase each child's projects together. Later, remove the portraits, retitle the display "A Pack of Outstanding Work," and exhibit a student-selected work sample with each crayon cutout.

Laura Mihalenko—Gr. 2, Truman Elementary School, Parlin, NJ

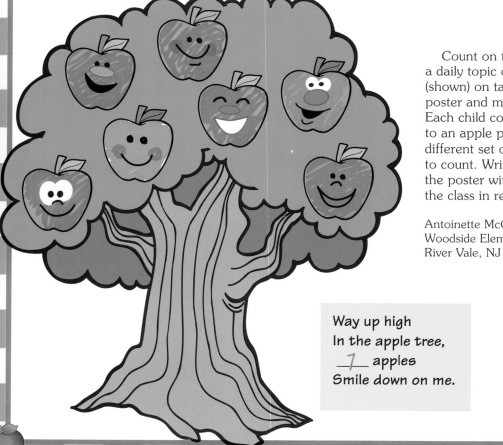

Count on this back-to-school display being a daily topic of discussion! Copy the rhyme (shown) on tagboard. Laminate the resulting poster and mount it near a large paper tree. Each child colors and adds facial features to an apple pattern (page 17). Display a different set of apples each day for students to count. Write the class-approved count on the poster with a wipe-off marker; then lead the class in reading the rhyme.

Antoinette McCoy
Woodside Elementary
River Vale, NJ

Way up high
In the apple tree,
___7___ apples
Smile down on me.

Soar into the new school year with this *eye-catching* display! Have each child illustrate his likeness on drawing paper trimmed to resemble the window of a plane. Mount the projects on a large paper plane that's being piloted by you. Mount the plane, the title, and several cloud cutouts labeled with student-dictated goals for the new school year. Looks like the sky's the limit!

Ann Galster, Ellicott Elementary, Colorado Springs, CO

Sprout self-confidence and camaraderie at this adorable garden! Mount the title and one colorful flower per child, plus a few extras for late enrollees. Have each child trace a template of a flower center onto skin-toned paper, cut out the circle, and then use construction paper, glue, and crayons to create her self-portrait. Showcase the projects as shown. Too sweet!

Misty Rios, E. W. Ward Elementary, Downey, CA

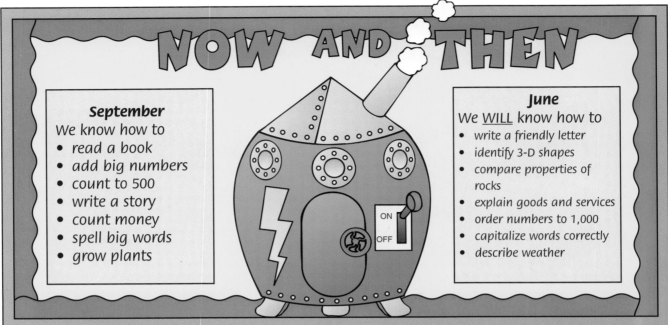

NOW AND THEN

September
We know how to
- read a book
- add big numbers
- count to 500
- write a story
- count money
- spell big words
- grow plants

June
We **WILL** know how to
- write a friendly letter
- identify 3-D shapes
- compare properties of rocks
- explain goods and services
- order numbers to 1,000
- capitalize words correctly
- describe weather

What does the future hold for your students? To find out the answer to that question, go right to the source! Mount the title and a time machine similar to the one shown. Then, under your students' guidance, prepare two lists: one that details what the students know right now and one that details what the students plan to know at the end of the school year. Showcase the completed lists at the display. The future looks bright!

Whitney Sherman, Seven Pines Elementary School, Sandston, VA

We've Been on the Move!

| Jose — Going to See Grandma | Stevie — The Shopping Mall | Jane — Fun at the Fair | Nadine — The Lake | Greg — Camping With Uncle Joe | Karim — The Beach! |

| Keiko — Bringing Our Puppy Home | Sam — The Airport | Shalita — Fun in Florida | Linda — Seeing My Dad |

This travel display is quite a sight! Ask each student to ponder the places she visited over the summer as she personalizes, colors, and cuts out a car-shaped paper topper (page 17). Then have her write and illustrate a story about one place she visited. Display the students' stories and paper toppers as shown. Invite students to continue their travels by reading about their classmates' trips!

adapted from an idea by Angie Kelley, Weaver Elementary School, Anniston, AL

Great things are created with teamwork, and this display is a perfect example! Mount a border and the phrase "Doing Our Part to Make It a Great." From poster board cut large letters to spell "YEAR!" Visually divide the letter cutouts into a class supply of puzzle pieces; then label each piece for a different student. Code the back of each letter cutout (for easy reassembly) before cutting it apart. Have each child decorate his puzzle piece. Then, with your youngsters' help, assemble and mount the puzzle pieces as shown. It's going to be a great year!

Mary Jo Kampschnieder
Howells Community Catholic School
Howells, NE

Create miles of smiles with this back-to-school display. Cover a bulletin board with white paper. A student uses assorted arts-and-crafts supplies to create her self-portrait on a construction paper oval. Then she mounts her self-portrait and precut letters spelling "ME" on a colorful rectangle. Display the projects in a checkerboard pattern, leaving room for the title near the top. You can count on plenty of students, parents, and staff members checking out this display!

Linda Macke, John F. Kennedy Elementary, Kettering, OH

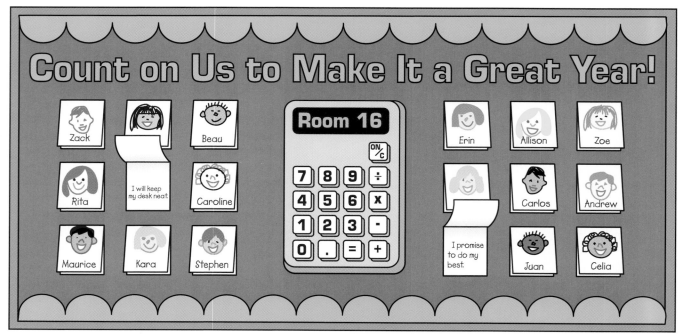

Count on Us to Make It a Great Year!

Zack · Beau · Rita · I will keep my desk neat. · Caroline · Maurice · Kara · Stephen

Room 16 — ON/C — 7 8 9 ÷ · 4 5 6 × · 1 2 3 - · 0 . = +

Erin · Allison · Zoe · I promise to do my best. · Carlos · Andrew · Juan · Celia

When it comes to promoting classroom cooperation, this display is unequaled! Mount the title and a labeled paper calculator. Have each child illustrate his likeness on the outside of a folded piece of white paper and sign his name. Ask him to write on the inside one way that he will contribute to the classroom community. Showcase students' work as desired. Impressive!

Jo Fryer, Kildeer Countryside School, Long Grove, IL

Meet a Wonderful Bunch!

Jana · B. J. · Pete · Tameka · Diana · Ben · Rachel · Mia · Joey · Justin · Marcy · Tina · Jolene · Caroline · Alec

Looking for a creative hallway welcome? Go grape! Have each student illustrate a favorite activity on a 3" x 4" piece of paper. Ask her to glue the illustration on a seven-inch purple construction paper circle and then write her name below it. Arrange students' work on a wall to resemble a bunch of grapes; then embellish and title the display as shown.

Linda B. West
Jefferson Elementary School
Winston-Salem, NC

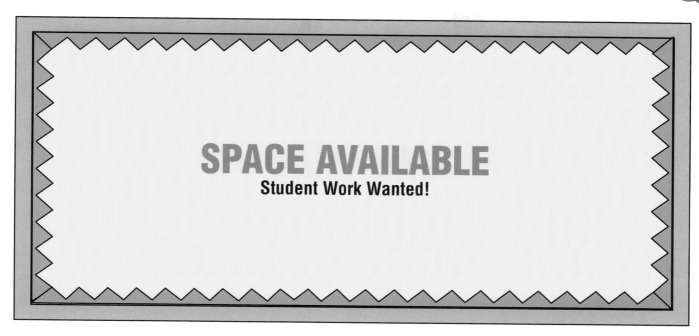

SPACE AVAILABLE
Student Work Wanted!

Here's a bulletin board that's a teacher's friend! Post the message shown and place a container of pushpins nearby. Ask each child to post at least one piece of work that represents her best efforts. Instruct students to update their work samples weekly to keep the display current. A highly motivating, child-centered bulletin board that's maintained by students—now that's a dream come true!

Linda Macke, John F. Kennedy Elementary, Kettering, OH

When students set their eyes on this "a-peel-ing" door decoration, you'll hear a chorus of oohs and aahs! Cover the door and an area of wall space around it with white paper. Mount a red apple-shaped border around the door, trim away unwanted white paper, and attach a paper leaf and stem. Personalize a seed cutout for each child. Mount the cutouts on the door and then use chalk or crayon to add apple core details. Wow! What an awesome apple!

Joyce R. Welford
Sandra Smith—Teacher Assistant
Leakesville Elementary School
Leakesville, MS

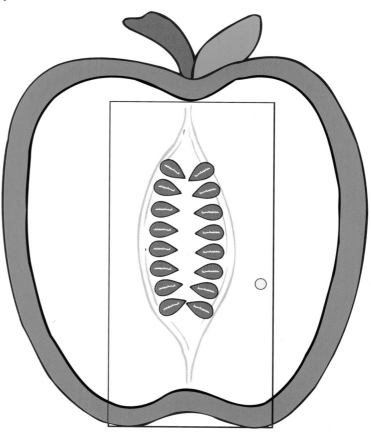

Monthly Banners

Create a visual diary of the school year! For each month, trim a sheet of poster board into a banner shape and then label it. Throughout the month, photograph your students engaged in a variety of activities. Trim several favorite photos, glue them to the banner, and display a student-dictated caption near each one. Add other mementos from the month as desired. Then display the project in the hallway for all to see. It looks like it's going to be a banner year!

Lynn Lupo-Hudgins
Austin Road Elementary
Stockbridge, GA

Smiles Galore

Here's a back-to-school display that's guaranteed to keep students smiling! Have each child trace a four-inch circle template onto skin-toned paper; then have him cut out the shape and decorate it to create a self-portrait. Mount the completed projects on a large numeral cutout that represents your grade level. Display the numeral along with die-cut letters that spell out "Second grade is '2-rrific'!" or "Third grade is '3-mendous'!"

Jo Fryer
Kildeer Countryside School
Long Grove, IL

Crayon Pattern

Use with "Introducing the Pack!" on page 10.

Apple Pattern

Use with the display on page 10.

Car Pattern

Use with "We've Been on the Move!" on page 12.

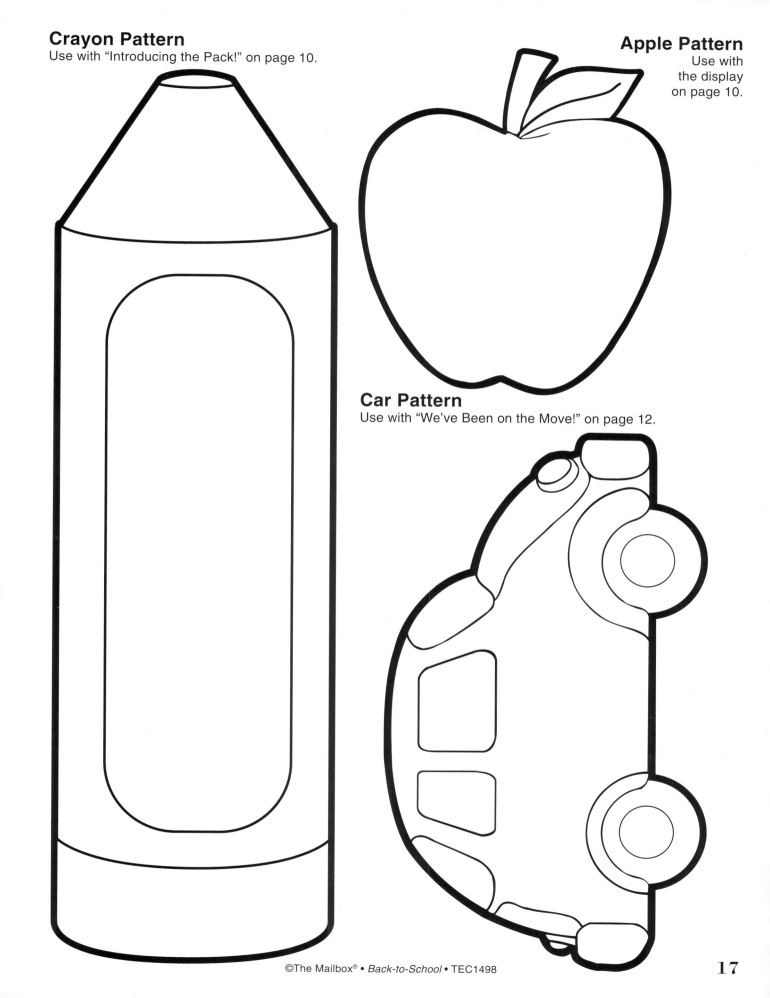

Bulletin Board Binder

No doubt you'll make a beeline for this binder of bulletin board ideas time and time again! Label a divider page for each month of the school year and then organize the divider pages in a three-ring binder. Behind each divider page, store any bulletin board ideas you have for that month. As you collect new ideas during the year, add them to the binder. If desired, also add photographs of your own classroom displays. You'll have an invaluable resource right at your fingertips!

Susan L. Nowlin—Gr. 2
R. C. Waters Elementary
Oak Harbor, OH

Bag of Borders

Organizing bulletin board borders in a shoe storage bag with clear pockets is a smart idea! Suspend the bag inside a closet door. Roll up your borders and store them in the clear pockets. Now you can find the border you need at a glance!

Debra Culpepper—Gr. 3
Cedar Road Elementary
Chesapeake, VA

Roll-a-Site

Before school begins organize your favorite Web addresses on a Rolodex rotary file. List each address and the topic the site covers on an individual card. Also add a short description of what can be found at the site. Then file the card alphabetically by topic in your rotary file. Store the card file and a pen or pencil near your classroom computer. Each time you discover another great Web site, complete a card for it and insert it into your file. The days of staring at a list of bookmarked sites and wondering what information is offered at each one are over! Now you can check your card file and easily put your finger on a Web address for the desired topic.

Jeannie Hinyard—Gr. 2
Welder Elementary School
Sinton, TX

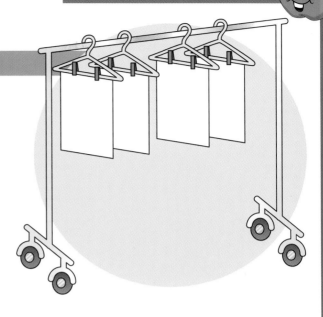

Timesaving Storage Tip

Save precious time throughout the year by organizing your teaching charts. Clip each chart to a hanger and then suspend the hanger from an inexpensive garment rack (available at discount stores). Organize the charts by subject, season, or kind. Store the rack in a desired classroom location. Each time you need a teaching chart, you'll know right where to look!

Janet S. Witmer
Harrisburg, PA

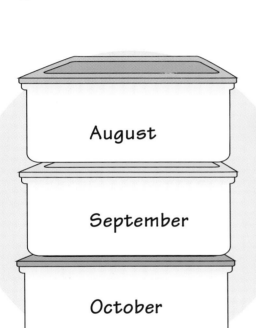

Storage by the Month

Here's another tip that saves you oodles of time during the school year! Label a large stackable container for each month of the school year. In each container, store bulletin board cutouts, learning center games, and other items that cannot be filed in a monthly file folder. When it's time to prepare for a new month, grab your monthly file and box and you're ready to get busy!

Penny Webster—Special Education
Crossroads Elementary School
Whitwell, TN

Fantastic Folders

Help your youngsters organize their papers with this simple pocket folder system. Have each student bring three pocket folders to school. Collect one of the folders and store it as a replacement. Have each student label one folder "Stay at School," label another folder "Take Home," and decorate them both. Explain to your students that schoolwork for collection at the end of each day should be placed in their school folders. Papers that need to be taken home should be placed in their home folders for review with a parent each night. (You may choose to include a parent sign-off sheet in each home folder.) Parents and students will agree that this organized approach is fantastic!

Margie Siegel—Gr. 2
Wren Hollow Elementary School
Ballwin, MO

Monthly Workmats

Protect desktops and strengthen calendar skills with monthly workmats! Each month have every child program a blank calendar grid for the current month and label it with family- and school-related events. Next, have him glue the calendar on a 12" x 18" sheet of construction paper, personalize the project, and add desired artwork. Laminate the completed mats. Ask students to work atop their mats when they use potentially messy supplies such as glue and paint. The end result is cleaner desktops and more calendar-related conversations!

Betty Klein
Sheridan Road School
Fort Sill, OK

Sticker Rings

Save time and minimize clutter by organizing your sticker collection on metal rings. Hole-punch the top of each sticker sheet as you sort the sheets by theme, holiday, or other desired criteria. Then bind each group of stickers onto a separate ring. Your days of sifting through miscellaneous stickers are over!

Heather Volkman—Grs. 1–2
Messiah Lutheran School
St. Louis, MO

Checkout System

Have you repeatedly wished for a checkout system for classroom library books? Take action! Enlist a group of student volunteers to glue a library pocket inside the front cover of each book. In each pocket insert a card labeled with the book's title. In the fall, glue library-card pockets labeled with your students' names (one pocket per child) to a piece of poster board and display the resulting poster. To check out a book from the classroom library, a child places its card into her personalized library pocket. A quick glance at the poster reveals which books the students are reading.

Faye Harris Bruce—Gr. 3
Water Valley Elementary
Water Valley, MS

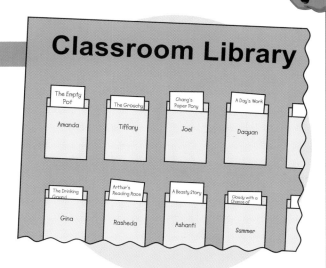

Classroom Library

Stick with this system, and maintaining an orderly library will be as easy as A, B, C! Gather a supply of paint sticks (often free where paint is sold) and personalize one stick per student. Each time a student removes a book from the classroom library, she leaves her personalized paint stick in its place. She then removes the stick when she returns the book to its original location.

Linda Macke—Gr. 2
John F. Kennedy School
Kettering, OH

Book Clips

If you use baskets to organize the books in your classroom library, this tip is for you! Store a class supply of personalized clothespins in your library. When a student selects a book to read, have him clip a personalized clothespin to the corresponding basket. When it's time to return the book, he'll know exactly where it belongs!

Melissa Meswick—Gr. 2
Parsons Elementary School
North Brunswick, NJ

Hook a Book

Taking a few minutes now to organize your book and tape sets will prepare you for fall, plus it encourages this year's students to revisit your collection. Place each book and its corresponding tape in a resealable plastic bag and then clip a clothespin hanger to the bag. Display a sheet of pegboard near your listening center. Insert inexpensive hooks into the pegboard and suspend each bag from a hook. Your students will be all ears!

Alisa T. Daniel
Ben Hill Primary
Fitzgerald, GA

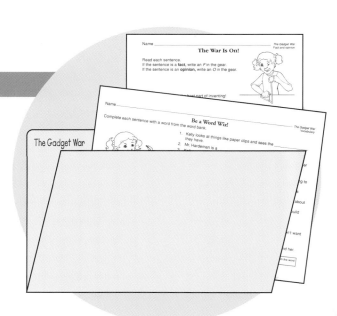

Literature Folders

Keep literature-related activities at your fingertips with this organizational system. Label a file folder for each story you plan to use with your students. When you find an idea or reproducible that relates to one of the stories, file a copy of it in the appropriate folder. You'll soon have several ideas per title. Writing lesson plans will be a snap, and you'll have a handy resource for substitute teachers.

Margarett Mendenhall
Mary Feeser Elementary School
Elkhart, IN

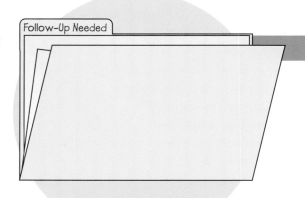

Follow-Up Folder

Providing individualized instruction just got easier! Keep a file folder labeled "Follow-Up Needed" on your desk. When a child's completed work indicates that he needs additional help with a skill, file his paper in the folder. Each time you have a few free minutes, select a paper from the folder and meet with that youngster. Spare minutes quickly become teachable moments!

Gina Marinelli—Gr. 2
Bernice Young Elementary
Burlington, NJ

Versatile Letters

Use recycled bulletin board letters to prepare a literacy center in a jiffy! When you replace a titled classroom display, save any unneeded letter cutouts. Place the letters at a center stocked with paper and pencils. Have students complete a variety of grade-appropriate tasks, such as putting the letters in alphabetical order, using the letters to make words, or writing a brainstormed list of words that begin with a selected letter. The possibilities are endless!

Kathleen Lasky
Pensacola, FL

Reusable Class Book

Stock a view binder with top-loading sheet protectors, and you have a class book that's easy to use and reuse! Simply insert a cover page into the plastic pocket on the front of the binder and then display students' work in the sheet protectors. This quick and easy approach to publishing eliminates the need for lamination, and it enables you to return each child's work. Better buy two or three binders! You'll be glad you did!

Sue Fichter—Gr. 2
St. Mary of the Woods
Chicago, IL

Schoolwide Memos

If your school saves paper by sending home schoolwide memos with just the oldest child in each represented family, try this! Attach a colorful sticker dot to the desk of each child who is to receive the paperwork. Then send home schoolwide memos with students who have the dots on their desks. Distributing papers by the dots definitely saves time!

Kelly Hanover—Gr. 2
Saint Edward School
Racine, WI

Notable Communication

Use this bright idea, and you can be sure that your notes to parents won't get lost in the shuffle! Keep a supply of vividly colored envelopes on hand. When you have a message or notice that requires immediate attention, tuck it in an envelope before giving it to the appropriate student to take home. Parents will recognize the colorful correspondence at a glance!

Sandy Preston—Gr. 2
Brockway Area Elementary School
Brockway, PA

Homework Helper

This organizational idea doubles as a homework incentive! Throughout the day, have each student place any homework assignments in a personalized folder for convenient transport home. Have him return the completed assignments in the folder and place the folder in an established homework box. When you check the homework, stamp the inside of the folder once for each completed assignment. After a student accumulates a predetermined number of stamps, recognize his homework efforts with a special note or privilege.

Debbie Sietsema—Gr. 2
Allendale Public School
Allendale, MI

Catch of the Day!

Fishing for a way to organize counters, markers, pens, and other supplies you use with the overhead projector? Try a tackle box! Purchase a tackle box with movable sections that can be customized to hold your items. Keep the box on the overhead projector cart, and you'll never have to cast around for supplies again!

Todd Helms—Gr. 2
Pinehurst Elementary
Pinehurst, NC

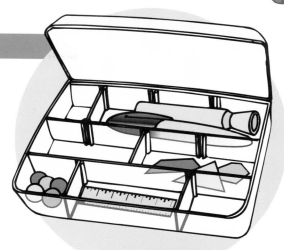

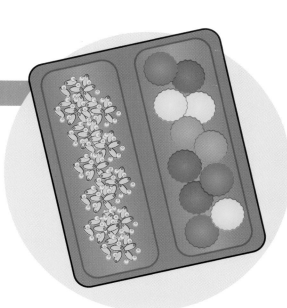

Oliver

Handy Pencil Holders

Here's an easy way to avoid interruptions caused by lost pencils. Attach one side of a small Velcro strip toward the eraser end of a child's pencil. Attach the other side of the Velcro strip to his desk nametag. Have the youngster adhere his pencil to his nametag when it's not in use. Now when he needs a pencil, he'll know exactly where to look!

Kelly Cox—Special Education
Rosedale Elementary
Middletown, OH

Art Organizer

Keep small art supplies orderly with this neat tip. Collect several plastic cookie and cracker trays that are divided into different compartments. Store craft items like sequins, beads, pom-poms, and tiny tissue paper scraps in the trays. You'll have easily accessible supplies that are neatly organized!

Martha Bronczek—Gr. 3
Bowers Elementary
Massillon, OH

Class Rules

1. Be kind.
2. Stay safe.
3. Follow directions.

Three Class Rules

One, two, three! Take this approach to identifying class rules, and three is all you need! Begin by asking students to brainstorm possible class rules. List their suggestions on an overhead or on the chalkboard. When the list is much too long for anyone to remember, suggest grouping the rules into categories. Three positively stated categories that will include most rules are "Be kind," "Stay safe," and "Follow directions." Lead students to this discovery and then post the class-created rules in a prominent location. Positive results are sure to follow!

Cheryl A. Wade—Gr. 2
Golden Springs Elementary School
Anniston, AL

Rules That Make Sense

Rather than present a set of class rules that may not make sense to students, gather students for a game of What Would You Do? To play, pose questions related to student behavior and classroom procedures, such as "What would you do if you had a question for the teacher?" and "What would you do if the fire alarm sounded?" Discuss all responses with the class and then guide students to identify the behavior or procedure that you feel is most appropriate for your classroom setting. List the resulting rules on a chart for future reference. Now that's a question-and-answer game that really teaches!

Darcy Gruber
Delawan, WI

What would you do if you had a question for the teacher?

Raise my hand!

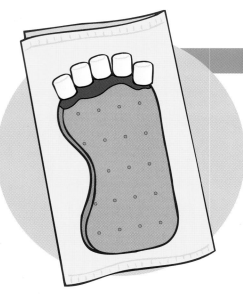

Marshmallow Toes

Here's a tasty first-week activity that leaves a lingering impression about acceptable hallway behavior. To begin, have each child use her five senses to investigate a large marshmallow. (Emphasize that marshmallows are soft and noiseless.) Next, instruct every child to nibble off each corner of a large graham cracker. Then have her nibble away a section near the middle of the cracker to create a shape that resembles a footprint. Finally, have each child use frosting to attach five mini marshmallow toes to the footprint. As the students eat their snacks, ask them to imagine softly walking down the hallway on marshmallow toes. Then invite them to practice these soft steps each time they enter the hallway.

Misti Craig
Campbellsville Elementary
Campbellsville, KY

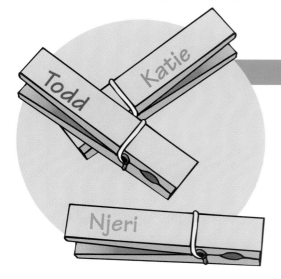

Lunchroom Behavior

Reduce behavior problems in the lunchroom with this positive plan. Personalize a clothespin for each child and then display the clothespins so they are easy for students to retrieve. As each child lines up for lunch, he collects his clothespin and clips it to his shirt sleeve. If he returns to the classroom after lunch with his clothespin in place, he earns one point for the class. If he is involved in a behavior-related incident and asked to surrender his clothespin, he earns no point. When a set number of points are earned, reward the class with extra recess time!

Jennifer Norman
Maplewood Elementary
Sunrise, FL

Pizza by the Slice

Reinforce fractions *and* motivate students to be on their best behavior! Draw a pizza shape on the chalkboard; then divide it into six or more equal slices. Each time you observe exemplary behavior, reward the class by coloring one pizza slice. Also announce the fraction that tells how much pizza is colored and write it near the pie. When the entire pizza is decorated, reward the class with a tasty snack of pizza-flavored Goldfish crackers. Then erase the toppings, reslice the pizza, and repeat the process. Yum!

Dawn Scott—Gr. 2
Baxter Elementary
Midlothian, TX

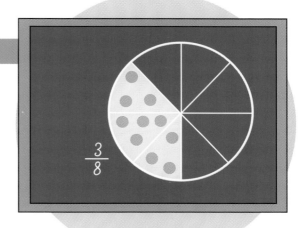

Doable Documentation

Take a practical approach to documenting student behavior. Write each child's name on a Post-it index tab. Attach each flag to a different page of a spiral notebook, leaving four blank pages between flags. Program each flagged page with family and medical information about the named student. Label each set of blank pages for the four quarters of the school year. To document student behavior, simply turn to the appropriate notebook page and then date and note your observation. Now that's doable!

Irene Thayer
Odebolt-Arthur Community School
Odebolt, IA

Hey, class! What do you say?
Who have you caught being good today?

Hey, [student's name]. What do you say?
Who have you caught being good today?

Caught Being Good!

This catchy chant promotes community within the classroom and helps refocus the class for the next task at hand. To establish a beat and ready the students, alternate between clapping your hands and patting your thighs. Students join in and then begin the chant (shown) on your cue, pausing to hear which student you call upon and sitting quietly while he responds. Students enjoy sharing the good deeds of their classmates, and they will occasionally catch a teacher being good too!

Laura Dickerson
Seawell Elementary School
Chapel Hill, NC

Can-Do Attitude

The piggies in David McPhail's *Those Can-Do Pigs* can do just about anything—even inspire your students to be can-do kids! To develop a can-do attitude in your class, read aloud McPhail's hilarious tale. Follow up by asking students to suggest positive school-related behaviors that they can do. Copy each statement on story paper and then distribute the papers for students to illustrate. Bind the completed pages between construction paper covers and title the book "The Can-Do Kids of Room [room number]." With a can-do attitude, anything is possible!

Julie Bulver—Gr. 2
Rice Elementary School
Des Moines, IA

The Can-Do
Kids of Room
A12

Jenna

Sunshine Basket

Show students that their good behavior brightens your day! Place a small basket within easy student reach. Each time you observe a student displaying exemplary behavior, ask her to personalize a small sun cutout and then drop it in the basket. At the end of each week, draw several names from the basket and reward each of these students with a small treat or happy note. Then empty the basket, and you're ready to reinforce positive behavior the following week. Let the sun shine in!

Gina Marinelli—Gr. 2
Bernice Young Elementary
Burlington, NJ

This pat on the back is for helping Zoey find her lunch ticket.

A Colorful Pat

How do you give a colorful pat on the back? Like this! Keep a colorful supply of hand-shaped cutouts at your desk. When a student deserves a pat on the back, briefly describe his accomplishment on a cutout and then tape it to the back of his shoulder. A child's self-esteem soars when he receives your pat on the back, and each time he's asked to explain the cutout he's wearing, it soars again!

Alesia Richards—Grs. K–5
Senseny Road Elementary
Winchester, VA

VIB Treasure Chests

Each week award a Very Important Buccaneer with a bounty of treasured compliments. Fold, staple, and decorate a sheet of 12" x 18" construction paper to make a pocketed treasure chest like the one shown. After the buccaneer of the week has been selected, give each of his classmates a pattern of a smiling coin. Ask each student to cut out the paper coin and label the back with a positive comment about the VIB of the week. Encourage students to write thoughtful messages, and explain that they have until noon on Friday (or another designated day and time) to complete the coins. Verify that each child has signed his coin before collecting them in the treasure chest. Then add a personalized coin yourself and use a yellow sticky dot to seal the chest before you present the treasure to the VIB. No doubt he'll be pleased with his good fortune!

Ann Marie Stephens
George C. Round Elementary School
Manassas, VA

You're a super artist! Sam

You're good at math. Jan

•1•2•3•4•5•

Give Me Five!

I'm on one.
The counting has begun!
I'm on two.
Where are you?
I'm on three.
Where should you be?
I'm on four—
Only one more!
Five!

•1•2•3•4•5•

Transitions by the Number

Looking for a simple way to prepare students for a new task? Use the provided poem to prompt youngsters to clear their work areas and give you their attention. They'll be ready in no time at all. You can count on it!

Jennifer Reno
Adolph Link Elementary
Elk Grove Village, IL

Ready to Begin

Here's an upbeat way to ready students for a new task. If it's September say, "One apple, two apples, three apples," adjusting the tempo of the phrase to allow sufficient time for students to ready themselves. Then snap your fingers twice, prompting a student response of "Johnny Appleseed!" Count pumpkins in October ("It's harvest time!"), Pilgrims in November ("We are thankful!"), and candles in December ("Happy holidays!"). Timely transitions are guaranteed!

Lynda Wiedenhaupt—Gr. 2
Oshkosh Christian School
Oshkosh, WI

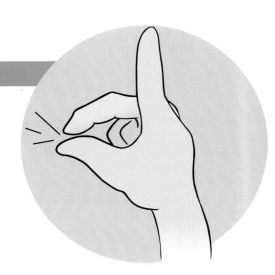

Buckle Up!

Get students in the learning habit with a visualization technique! Ask each child to imagine her desk as a car (or spaceship or airplane) that takes exciting learning journeys. Suggest that the greatest learning occurs when a driver is buckled in with an imaginary seat belt. Each morning have students enact buckling up for the day's learning adventures. During the day, give buckle-up reminders to quicken transitions or refocus your youngsters' attention. Vroom!

Diana Cassidy—Gr. 2
Ascension Catholic School
Melbourne, FL

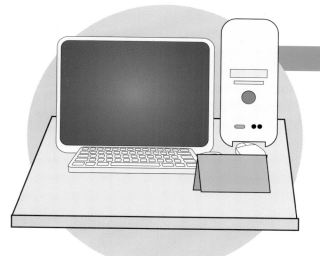

Computer Lab Queries

Implement this three-step approach to answering computer-related questions, and there's an excellent chance students will use it throughout the school day! Ask that during lab time each child try first to answer his own question. If he cannot, he asks a classmate for help. If his question is still unanswered, he displays a bright orange card (or something similar) to request help from the teacher. Along with fostering a user-friendly lab, you'll boost the self-esteem of your students!

Cori Collins—Computer Teacher K–5
St. Mary, St. Margaret Mary, and St. Gabriel Schools
Neenah-Menasha, WI

Textbook Checkout

Encourage students to take better care of their textbooks with this easy-to-implement management system. Before school begins, make a 3" x 5" form that lists each subject for which a student will have an assigned textbook. Later, when you've distributed the textbooks, have each child write the numbers of her textbooks on a copy of the form. Verify each student's form and then ask her to sign it. If desired, have each child cut out her completed form and mount it on a provided index card. Collect the forms and store them in alphabetical order. When the end of the year rolls around, or a student moves away, you can easily account for any missing or damaged books.

Louis A. Kucinski—Gr. 3
Citrus Park Elementary School
Tampa, FL

Textbooks
Reading _12_
Spelling _8_
Math _6_
Science _10_
Signed: *Jenny Curtis*

Name	Assignment	Due date	Date turned in
Bryton Lee	Manners Booklet	Aug. 28	Aug. 29
Sarah Edwards	Manners Booklet	Aug. 28	

Homework Strategy

Start the school year with this proven homework strategy, and you'll have fewer homework-related worries. Program the first several pages of a spiral notebook like the page shown. Keep the resulting homework notebook at your desk. When a student does not complete a homework assignment, she writes her name, a description of the assignment, and the due date on the first available line in the notebook. She completes her entry when she finishes the homework. In addition to providing you with a handwritten record of homework habits, students quickly understand that completing homework is their responsibility.

Susan Hearon—Gr. 3
All Saints' Episcopal Day School
Florence, SC

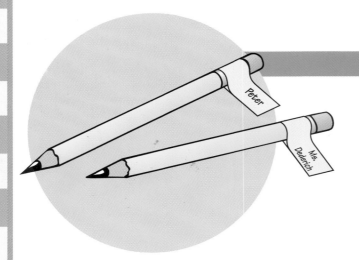

Missing Pencil Solution

Do pencils seem to disappear in your classroom? Try this! Secure a narrow adhesive label (such as a file folder label) around the top of a pencil to make a flag. Label the flag with the name of the owner or the center in which the pencil belongs. Any stray pencils can be easily returned to their rightful places!

Elizabeth Dederich—Gr. 2
Westwood Elementary
Springdale, AR

Pencil Sharpener Solution

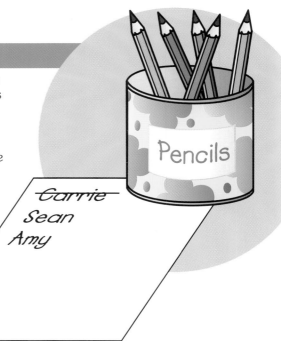

Here's an easy way to avoid interruptions caused by students sharpening their pencils. Place a container of sharpened pencils and a sign-out sheet near the class sharpener. If a student suddenly finds herself needing to sharpen her pencil at an inappropriate time, she signs one out. Later, during an approved time, she sharpens her pencil, sharpens and returns the one she borrowed, and crosses off her name. No more interruptions!

Kim Noviello—Gr. 3
JFK Primary Center
New Castle, PA

Tidy Desks

Encourage neat and clean student desks with a small stuffed animal (or two)! Tell students that the animal's natural habitat is a clean and organized desk. Explain that each evening the critter will examine the inside and outside of every desk to find a clean home for the following school day. Invite the child whose desk is chosen to include the stuffed critter in his school activities for the day. Tidy desks will be all around!

Maya Kobashigawa—Gr. 3
Burton Valley Elementary
Lafayette, CA

Daily Lineup

Keep students lining up in an orderly fashion day after day! Arrange the students' desks in five groups and name each group for a different weekday. A group lines up first during its namesake day. The first group is followed in line by the group named for the next weekday, and then the next, and so on until all groups are in line. With this systematic approach, lining up quickly and quietly soon becomes a habit!

Pat Hart—Gr. 2
C. A. Henning School
Troy, IL

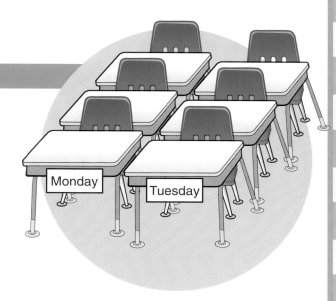

Student Work Folders

Setting aside time before the school day starts to make a class set of work folders is a wise investment. You'll profit each time a child removes an unfinished paper from his folder and completes it without a reminder from you! Have each child personalize and decorate a colorful file folder. Laminate the folders for durability and, if you prefer, staple or securely tape the sides of each folder to form a pocket. Explain to students that only unfinished school work goes inside the folders. Also clarify that a student must have an empty work folder before he engages in free-time activities. If work remains in the folder at the end of the day, it becomes homework. Students know from the start that finishing their work is top priority!

Ann McGregor—Gr. 2
Emily Carr Public School
London, Ontario, Canada

The Back-to-School Express

A Trainload of First-Day Activities

Here's just what you need to start off the school year right on track—a trainload of first-day ideas from our subscribers! With this precious cargo, it's full steam ahead for a fabulous school year. All aboard!

Teacher Tales

Sharing information about yourself is a great way to help students feel at home in their new surroundings. Gather several photos that span your life. Mount each snapshot on an 8½" x 11" sheet of paper, and write a concise and easy-to-read caption on the page. Slide each completed page into a plastic protector. Arrange the pages in chronological order before placing them in a three-ring binder. Add a title and desired decorations to the cover of the binder; then use the resulting autobiography to introduce yourself on the first day of school. Your students' interest will be piqued, and there's a good chance they'll be eager to share something about themselves too!

This is my cat, K.C. He is soft and cuddly.

Laura Mihalenko—Gr. 2
Truman Elementary School
Parlin, NJ

Colorful Introductions

Brighten up first-day introductions with this colorful activity. Choose a different color of crayon for each child in your class and place one crayon of this color in each of two containers. Gather the class in a large circle and distribute the crayons in one container. To begin the introductions, remove a crayon from the second container. Announce the color of the crayon and ask the student who is holding the same crayon color to tell the class her name and something about herself. Continue in this manner until each child has introduced herself. In no time at all, your students will have a colorful spectrum of new friends!

Sandy Wiele—Gr. 2
Peoria Christian School
Peoria, IL

100 Days

Set the stage for a 100th Day celebration with a journal-writing activity that really counts! To make a journal for each student, bind 50 pages of story paper between construction paper covers. On the first day of school, have each student personalize the covers of his journal and glue a copy of a hundreds chart inside the front cover. Near the end of the day, have each student open his journal to the first blank page. Instruct him to write the day's date in the top left corner of the page and the number of days school has been in session (1) in the top right corner. Then, on the same page, have each student write and illustrate a story about his school day. Finally, have the student color the corresponding day (1) on the hundreds chart.

Each school day have the students make an entry in their journals. Then, as part of your 100th Day celebration, invite students to read aloud their favorite journal entries. You can count on this idea to reinforce number concepts as well as reading and writing skills!

Stefanie Wilde
Plymouth Elementary School
Plymouth Meeting, PA

Hear Ye! Hear Ye!

Usher in a banner year with these noble student introductions! Enlarge the coat of arms pattern on page 40 to a desired size; then make student copies on white construction paper. Have each student write his name on the provided line and then complete each section of the pattern by providing the requested information and a related illustration. Next, have each child cut out his pattern, mount it on colorful construction paper, and trim the colored paper to create an eye-catching border. Display each student's coat of arms on a bulletin board titled "Hear Ye! Hear Ye! Read All About Our Class!"

Kelly A. Lu—Gr. 2
Berlyn School
Ontario, CA

First-Day Jitters

Your students' first-day jitters will quickly disappear with this hands-on activity! Use the recipe shown to make a class supply of play dough; then divide the dough into equal-size student portions. To prepare each portion, poke a deep hole in the dough, squeeze two to four drops of food coloring inside, and carefully reshape the dough, sealing the food coloring inside. Distribute the dough on the first day of school and ask each student to knead his portion. As the students are working, ask them if they have ever seen play dough change color. Then tell them that you think when this happens it means that a great school year lies ahead. Your classroom will echo with cries of delight when students see their play dough portions change color right before their eyes!

To extend the activity, ask each child to create a shape from his play dough that reveals one of his interests or hobbies. Invite students to take turns telling their classmates about the shapes they made; then have each student store his portion of dough inside a resealable plastic bag. The dough can then be taken home or stored at school for future use.

Melinda Phillips—Gr. 2
Donehoo Advanced Technology School
Glencoe, AL

First-Class Summer Memories

Memories of summer arrive special delivery with this postcard project! To prepare for the first-day project, illustrate one side of a large, white index card (unlined) to show a fond summer memory. Program the opposite side of the card to resemble a real postcard by writing a note to the class about your memory, addressing the card, drawing a stamp in the top right corner, and adding a desired postmark. On the first day of school, share the postcard you created; then ask each student to create a postcard about her favorite summer memory. For best results, draw a divider line and address lines on one side of a large, blank index card for each student. Also write on the chalkboard the address that you'd like each student to copy on her card.

To display the cards, hole-punch the center top of each card. Thread a length of yarn through the hole and tie the yarn ends. Then suspend the card from a pushpin inserted into a bulletin board titled "First-Class Summer Memories!"

Patti Hirsh—Gr. 3
Casis Elementary School
Austin, TX

Play Dough Recipe
(Makes about 24 student portions.)

Ingredients:
6 c. flour
3 c. salt
6 tbsp. cooking oil
6 c. water
4 tbsp. cream of tartar

Directions:
Mix the dry ingredients in a large cooking pan. Add the oil and water. Cook and stir the mixture over medium heat until it pulls away from the sides of the pan. Knead the dough; then store it in an airtight container.

Gullig, McKenzie
1. I have a dog, a cat, and a fish.
2. I have a lot of friends.
3. I like to ride my bike.
4. I like to play sports like baseball and basketball.
5. My mom is a teacher.
6. I like to write.

"Verse-atile" Posters

These personalized posters will speak volumes about your class! Before school starts, send a letter to parents requesting that their children bring five or six photos to school on the first day. Ask that the snapshots show the children and their family members and friends. Explain in the letter that the photos will be used for a get-acquainted project and that they will be returned taped to a decorative poster.

To make her poster, a student completes a construction paper copy of the poem on page 41, cuts it out, and glues it to the center of a colorful piece of poster board. Then she uses markers and large letters to write her name across the top of the poster board. Next, she tapes her photos to the poster board and uses colorful markers to add other desired decorations. When the posters are complete, encourage each student to share her work with the class. Then display the projects and the title "Meet the Students in Our Class!" on a bulletin board. The posters are a great way to promote student enthusiasm and friendships. And as an added bonus, you'll have created an engaging display for open house!

Cheryl Wade—Gr. 2
Golden Springs Elementary School
Anniston, AL

Who's Who Glossary

This first-day activity will be referred to all year long! Explain that the first project of the year is to make a who's who glossary that includes an entry for each student and yourself. To make his glossary entry, a student illustrates himself on a two-inch square of white construction paper. Then he glues his illustration in the top right corner of a lined 5" x 8" index card. Next, the student writes his full name (last name first, if desired) on the top line of the card, and he numbers and writes several sentences about himself on the lines that follow. He then glues his completed card to a 6" x 9" piece of colorful construction paper.

To assemble the project, create front and back covers from two 6" x 9" sheets of construction paper. Laminate the covers and the glossary entries for durability; then arrange the pages in alphabetical order between the covers. Bind the project so that additional pages (created by new students) can be added throughout the school year. In addition to initial student interest, the resulting glossary will be a great resource for new enrollees and for classroom visitors as they learn who's who. In fact, there's an excellent chance that the glossary will be the most well-read reference in your classroom library!

Connie Pinegar—Gr. 3
Mitchellville Elementary
Mitchellville, IA

Name Puzzles

Students will delight in creating and piecing together these personalized puzzles. Use colorful markers and large letters to write each child's name on a large, white, unlined index card. Then have each child use crayons to decorate the personalized side of her card before cutting the card into a designated number of puzzle pieces. Ask each child to assemble her puzzle; then give her a resealable plastic bag in which to store her puzzle pieces. Periodically throughout the day, ask each child to trade puzzles with a different classmate. After the students have assembled their classmates' puzzles, have them return the puzzles to their owners. By the day's end, each child will have met—and learned the names of—several of her new classmates!

Sue Ring
Fairlane Christian School
Dearborn Heights, MI

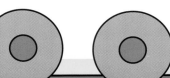

K is for playing kickball with my friends.

The ABCs of Summer

Make a splash with this big-book project! Ask students to brainstorm words that bring to mind their summertime activities. Write their ideas on the chalkboard, grouping together words that have the same beginning letters. Have each child choose a different alphabet letter and complete the following sentence near the top of a 12" x 18" sheet of drawing paper: "[Alphabet letter] is for [a corresponding word or phrase from the class list]." Then have each student illustrate his page using crayons or markers.

To assemble the big book, enlist your youngsters' help in alphabetizing the pages. Then hole-punch the students' work and two slightly larger pieces of poster board. Use metal rings to bind the pages between the poster board covers. Title the class big book "The ABCs of Summer" and place it in your classroom library for further reading enjoyment. Invite interested students to create additional pages for the book (perhaps for any alphabet letters that were not represented) during free time.

Whitney Sherman
Seven Pines Elementary School
Sandston, VA

Class,
I am sorry that I missed you in the office. I am on my way to the library. Maybe I will see you there!
Love,
Clifford

First-Day Reading

What could make students more proud than to show off their reading skills on the first day of school? To prepare for this activity, cut out a variety of familiar words and phrases from discarded newspapers, magazines, or product wrappers. Display the cutouts for your students' perusal. Then ask each child to choose three cutouts that she recognizes and glue them onto a sheet of construction paper. Invite each child to read aloud her word collection; then use a safety pin to attach a colorful copy of the reader's ribbon on page 40 to her clothing. Each young reader will surely burst with pride when she shares her first-day achievement with her family members!

Julie Bulver
Rice Elementary
Des Moines, IA

Where, Oh Where Has That Big Dog Gone?

Searching for a big red pooch is a perfect way to acquaint students with the school and staff members. Create a series of messages from Clifford the Big Red Dog. Each message should be written from a different school location. Explain that Clifford is searching for the wonderful students in your class, and end with a clue about the school location he will visit next. Write the first message as if the pooch had come by the classroom while you and your students were out. The next-to-last message should state that the canine is headed back to your class-room, and the final message should express regret for once again missing the youngsters. Copy each message on a paper bone (see the pattern on page 41). Hide the first clue in the classroom; then deliver the remaining bone cutouts to the appropriate school locations. Ask a neighboring colleague to deliver the final message to your classroom—along with a plate of bone-shaped sugar cookies and a Clifford puppet or stuffed animal—after the search has begun.

To begin the escapade, discover the first clue from Clifford shortly after you and your students return to the classroom after lunch, recess, or another outing. As you and your youngsters travel through the school, introduce the staff members you see along the way. No doubt students will have a "paws-itively" grand time tracking down Clifford!

Tina Bassett
J. R. Watson Elementary School
Auburn, IN

Classroom Treasure Hunt

Yo-ho! Welcome your new crew on board with a treasure hunt! Draw a simple classroom map; then label a variety of classroom locations and make an X on each one. Duplicate the map on manila paper for each student. To achieve a look of authenticity, either carefully tear the edges of each map or use a lighter to sear them. Then roll each map into a tube and tie a length of string or yarn around it. Next, decorate a large box to resemble a treasure chest and deposit the rolled maps inside. Also place a supply of adhesive stars at each classroom location marked on the map.

A student removes a map from the treasure chest and uses it to find the classroom locations marked. At each classroom location, he affixes a star to the corresponding point on his map. Your youngsters are certain to have a swashbuckling time exploring the classroom! And they'll each have a star-studded classroom map to share with family members.

Mary Grace Ramos—Gr. 2
Pinewood Acres School
Miami, FL

Name-o

Classroom introductions are a snap with this getting-acquainted game. Give each child a 5 x 5 grid, a list of student names, and 25 game markers—beans, buttons, paper squares, etc. (If you have fewer than 25 students, add your name and the names of other staff members to the list until it equals or exceeds 25.) Then have each student create a playing card by copying a different name from the list in each blank space on his grid.

To play, randomly call out the names from your list. If the name called is on a student's playing card, he covers the space with a game marker. After students have marked their boards, ask the youngster whose name was called to stand and tell his classmates something about himself. (You will need to provide information about any staff member whose name is called.) The first student to cover five squares in a vertical, horizontal, or diagonal row declares, "Name-o," and reads each name in his completed row. For an added challenge, ask the game winner to repeat one thing he learned about each person he names. Continue playing the game until you have called each name on the list one or more times. No doubt your youngsters will think this name game is a real winner!

Pamela Reifsneider—Associate Teacher
Newtown Friends School
Newtown, PA

History in the Making

Students will be thrilled to complete these time-capsules! To make a time capsule, a student personalizes and decorates a medium-size brown paper bag. Then she puts the following items in the bag: a length of string that equals her height, a self-portrait, a short poem that she copied in her best handwriting, and an interest inventory that she completed about herself. Staple each bag closed; then ask each child to deposit her resulting time capsule in a large box that you have provided for this purpose. Then, with great fanfare, securely seal the box. Later store the box out of sight. At the end of the year, reintroduce the box, open it, and return the time capsules to the students. Your youngsters will enjoy traveling back in time, and they'll be proud of the progress that they've made during the school year.

Debbie Fly
Birmingham, AL

Something Special

This first-day strategy eases the transition between home and school. Before the start of school, send a letter to your students' parents. In the letter, request that on the first day of school each child bring a special item—small in size—from home. Explain that each child will be asked to tell his classmates something about the item he brings.

Soon after the students arrive, gather them on the floor in a large circle. In turn, have each child show his classmates the item he brought from home and tell them about it. A student without a special item may talk about his favorite interests or pastimes. At the conclusion of the activity, ask students to display the items they brought from home in a special classroom location for the remainder of the day. The comfort and anticipation associated with the special items may actually reduce first-day anxieties!

Stefanie Wilde
Plymouth Elementary School
Plymouth Meeting, PA

Next Stop: Literature Station

Check out this specially engineered collection of school-related literature! It's just the ticket for keeping your first-class passengers on track with reading!

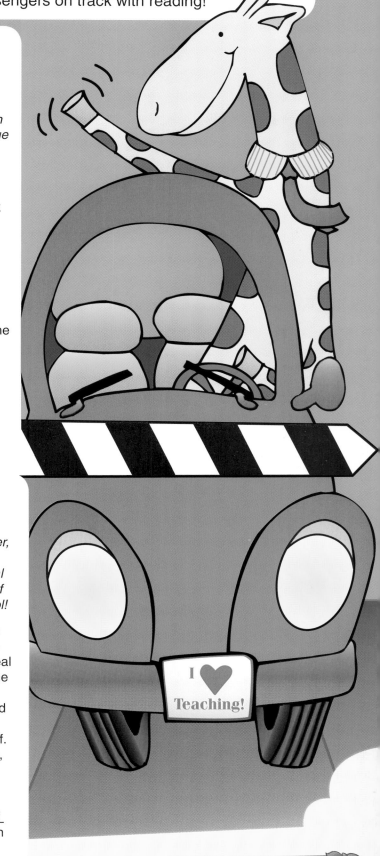

Miss Nelson Is Missing!
Written by Harry Allard & Illustrated by James Marshall

Miss Nelson's unruly students are eager to have a substitute teacher so that they can goof off all day long and do as little schoolwork as possible. Or so they think! Even in her own "absence," Miss Nelson skillfully teaches her students the value of respect and hard work.

This thought-provoking story about a teacher's creative approach to keeping her unruly class in line may teach your youngsters a thing or two! Prior to reading the story aloud, ask students to brainstorm qualities of a great teacher. List their ideas on the chalkboard under the heading "Great Teacher." At the conclusion of the story, ask students to recall the qualities that Miss Nelson believes great students should have. List these ideas on the chalkboard under the heading "Great Students." Then, under your students' direction, write the best of both these lists in a third list titled "World's Best Class." Guide students to understand how an entire class (including the teacher) can work together to exemplify the qualities that are listed. Reviewing classroom expectations and setting goals in this manner will surely make the grade!

Debbie Erickson—Grs. 2–3 Multiage
Waterloo Elementary School
Waterloo, WI

I Don't Want to Go Back to School
Written & Illustrated by Marisabina Russo

It's a child's worst back-to-school nightmare—a mean teacher, a class full of strangers, a wrong answer, a missed bus stop. Young Ben, about to begin the second grade, has his personal fears fed by his thorn-in-the-side big sister. But in spite of all of Ben's worrying, he has a perfectly wonderful first day at school!

Because the happy outcome of this delightful story will help put your youngsters at ease, make plans to read it early in the day. At the conclusion of the story, encourage students to reveal their worries about the first day of school. List their ideas on the chalkboard, and provide comfort and reassurance as needed. Then, near the end of the day, write a second student-generated list on the chalkboard that features first-day highlights. Next, have each child visually divide a sheet of drawing paper in half. On the left half of his paper, ask the student to copy, complete, and illustrate the following sentence: "Before school started I was worried [worries about the first day]." On the right half of his paper, have the student copy, complete, and illustrate this sentence: "Now that school has started, [feelings at the end of the day]." Have students take their papers home and use them to tell family members about their first day at school.

Coat of Arms Pattern
Use with "Hear Ye! Hear Ye!" on page 35.

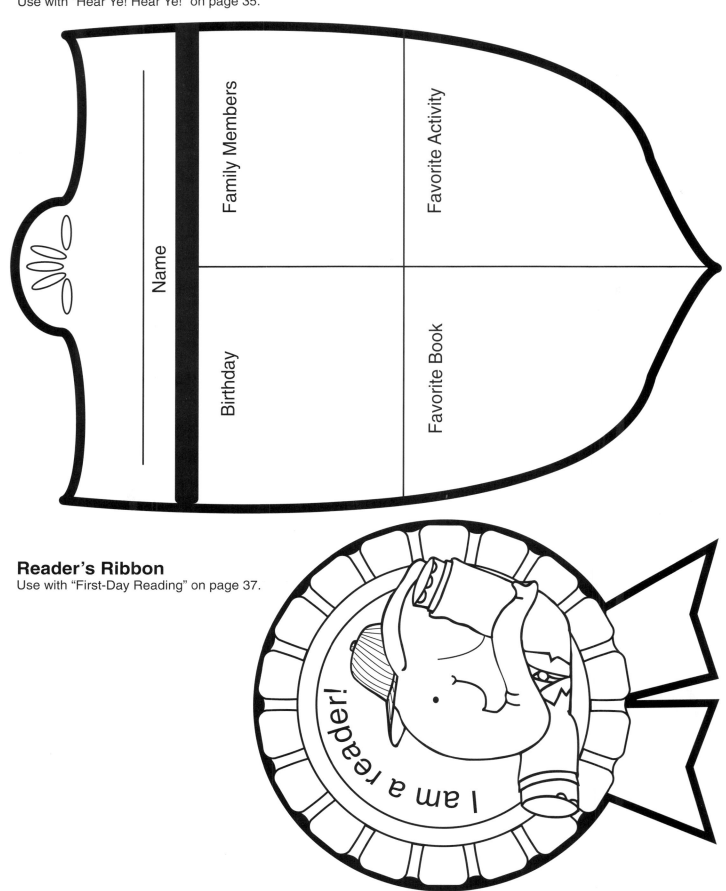

Name

Family Members

Favorite Activity

Birthday

Favorite Book

Reader's Ribbon
Use with "First-Day Reading" on page 37.

I am a reader!

I am _____.

Come read about me!

I was born _____.

I was a cute baby!

I have a friend named _____.

We play in all kinds of weather.

Whenever you see us,

We'll be together.

I like _____.

I really do.

I don't like _____.

How about you?

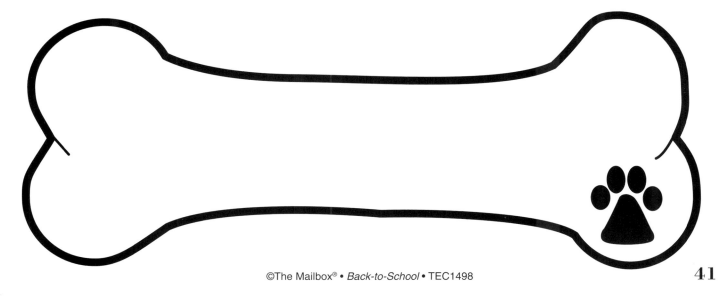

'Tis the Season for... Back-to-School!

Begin the new school year with these creative cross-curricular ideas!

ideas contributed by Kay Baker, Woodland Elementary, Emporium, PA

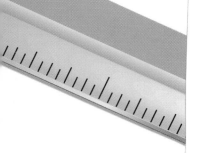

CLASSROOM MANAGEMENT

All Aboard!

Help your students start the year on the right track with this specially engineered display! Share the provided poem with students; then prompt a discussion to explore the importance of class rules. Next, write a student-generated list of rules on the chalkboard. With students' help, combine similar ideas and shorten the list. Write each agreed-upon rule on a separate boxcar that you have fashioned from a 9" x 12" sheet of construction paper. Prepare a simple engine from construction paper. Then assemble the train on a classroom wall, as shown, so that each car forms a pocket. To complete the display, give each youngster a person-shaped cutout. Have her embellish it to make a self-likeness. Tuck the completed artwork into the boxcars, adding additional cars for the precious cargo as necessary. All aboard!

Full Steam Ahead!

School is beginning. Welcome back!
Let's get started on the right track.
A few class rules are what we need
To help make sure we all succeed.

Use kind words.

Take turns.

Treat others as you would like to be treated.

Be a good listener.

WRITING

Front-Page News

Here's a newsworthy way to inform parents about the first week of school! Each student writes about the week's events on an eight-inch square of writing paper. Then he glues his writing near the bottom of a quarter page of newspaper. He uses a red marker to write a headline above his work. To create a self-likeness, he makes a face from a seven-inch construction paper circle and provided arts-and-crafts supplies. He uses construction paper to make two hands, a pair of pants, and two shoes. Then he assembles his project as shown. Encourage each youngster to take his work home to give his family the scoop on school!

School Opens!

This week was fun! I made a new friend. His name is Jordan. We tried the new playground equipment. It was cool! My teacher is nice. She let me use the computer. She said that we will use it a lot this year.

PROBLEM SOLVING

First Things First!

Logical reasoning is in order! Review your typical classroom schedule with students. Explain that a schedule helps a classroom run smoothly and lets students know what to expect. Invite students to share their ideas about what might happen if a teacher does not have a schedule in place. Then ask each student to complete a copy of the reproducible on page 44 to help one busy teacher get her schedule in order.

Ms. Collins

My birthday is in _____ .

My favorite color is _____ .

I like to eat _____ .

Interesting Introduction

Use this class activity to introduce yourself to students, and you'll learn about their decoding skills in the process! In advance, write several sentences about yourself on a sheet of chart paper using the format shown. Cover the key word in each sentence with a sticky note.

To begin, lead the class in reading the first sentence. Ask students to guess the covered word. Next, reveal the first letter of the word. Invite students to modify their guesses or make new guesses based on this clue. Then uncover the next letter or two. Repeat the process until students correctly identify the word and its spelling. Continue with the remaining sentences in the same manner. To follow up, invite each student to choose a topic from the chart and tell the class a corresponding fact about himself. Now that's a nifty get-acquainted idea!

MATH

Next Stop, School!

Math skills and a bit of luck make this partner game a winner! Give each twosome crayons, a copy of the gameboard on page 45, and four number cubes. Have each player initial a different bus on the gameboard. To begin, each player rolls two cubes. She adds the numbers shown on the tops of her cubes. The player who has the greater sum colors the first space on her road. If the players have the same sum, neither player colors a space. The game continues until one player reaches the school and is declared the winner!

SOCIAL STUDIES

Off to School!

Give students a glimpse of school in Africa! Show students the cover of *Where Are You Going, Manyoni?* by Catherine Stock and read the title aloud. Invite them to predict the setting and the answer to the title question. Read the story aloud to check students' predictions. Then share the author's note and wildlife information at the conclusion of the book. Point out Zimbabwe on a map or globe for clarification.

During a second reading of the story, ask students to pay particular attention to the things Manyoni sees and does before school. Then give each student a blank Venn diagram. Have him complete it to compare Manyoni's school morning routine with his own. Ask students to refer to their diagrams as you lead a class discussion about the noted similarities and differences.

School Mornings

Manyoni — Aaron

Manyoni: porridge, walks, baobab trees, baboons barking, long walk, lots of animals

Shared: birds, breakfast, recess, jump rope, friends

Aaron: cereal, toast, bus, pine trees, dogs barking, short ride, lots of cars

First Things First!

Ms. Place needs your help. She lost today's schedule!

Cut on the dotted lines.

Read the clues.

Put the subjects in order. Glue them in place.

Today's Schedule	
1.	
2.	
3.	
4.	
5.	
6.	
7.	
8.	

Clues

Art is between math and spelling.

Math is second.

Social studies is right before science.

Science is next to last.

Music is later than writing.

Writing is not first.

math	science	reading	art
music	social studies	writing	spelling

Note to the teacher: Use with "First Things First!" on page 42.

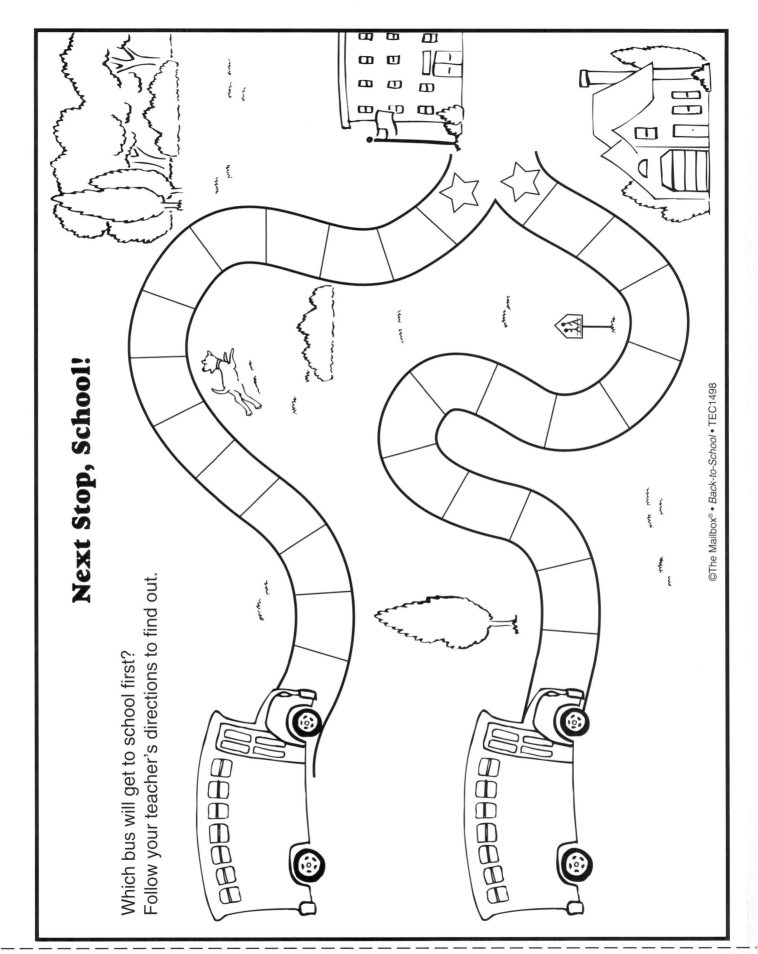

Next Stop, School!

Which bus will get to school first?
Follow your teacher's directions to find out.

©The Mailbox® • *Back-to-School* • TEC1498

Note to the teacher: Use with "Next Stop, School!" on page 43.

45

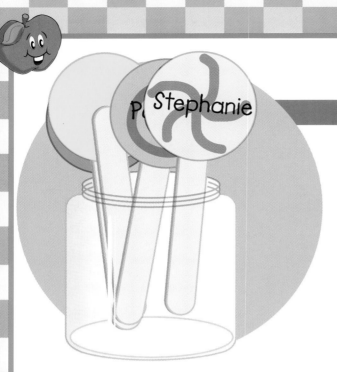

Sweet Comments

These lovely lollipops encourage students to learn about their classmates' positive qualities. To make her lollipop, a student personalizes and decorates a four-inch construction paper circle; then she glues the circle near the top of a tongue depressor. Store the lollipops in a plastic jar. During the first few weeks of school, gather students in a circle and distribute the lollipops, making sure no child receives her own. Ask each child, in turn, to share with the class something she has learned and especially likes about the classmate whose lollipop she is holding. Then collect the lollipops and store them for future rounds.

Denise Mason
Port Reading School
Port Reading, NJ

In the Cards

Invite students to drop anchor at this friendship center and play a Concentration partner game called I Like! To make a game, write a phrase from the provided list on each of two blank cards. Do the same for seven more phrases (for a total of 16 cards). If desired, place identical stickers on the backs of all 16 cards and laminate the cards for durability. Then store the cards in a resealable plastic bag at the center. Make as many card sets as desired.

To play the game, a pair of students scrambles the cards in one set and then arranges them facedown. Player 1 turns over two cards. If the cards are a match, she reads the phrase to her partner, adds "I like," and completes the phrase. Then she keeps the cards and turns over two more cards. If the cards are not a match, she turns the cards facedown again and Player 2 takes his turn. Play continues in this manner until all cards are matched. Students have fun playing the familiar game and learning about each other. Surely new friendships are in the cards!

adapted from an idea by Sarah Saia
Wilmington, NC

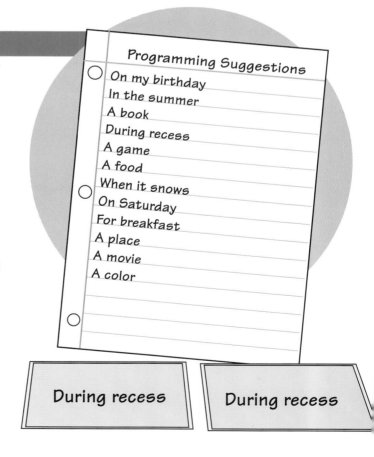

Programming Suggestions

On my birthday
In the summer
A book
During recess
A game
A food
When it snows
On Saturday
For breakfast
A place
A movie
A color

During recess

During recess

Pal Posters

Promote friendship and build self-esteem with a poster-making activity. To make his poster, a child uses large letters to write his name at the top of a 12" x 18" sheet of white construction paper. Below his name he illustrates his self-likeness. Next, he writes on his poster five activities he enjoys and five words that describe his personality. (Provide assistance as needed.) Set aside time for each child to share his poster with his peers. Then exhibit the projects in a school hallway where other potential pals can take a peek.

adapted from an idea by Kirsten S. Reynolds—Gr. 2
South Elementary School
Andover, MA

Something Special

What exactly is in a name? Help your students find out with this intriguing investigation! First, tell students that *every* name is special. Further explain that a name might be special because of its meaning, origin, family significance, or a variety of other factors. Then share a book that explores unusual names, such as *Chrysanthemum* by Kevin Henkes or *The Name Jar* by Yangsook Choi.

To help students uncover the stories behind their names, place a reference with the meanings and origins of names in a center. Arrange for each student to visit the center to research his first name. Also encourage him to talk with his family members about his name. He might ask them how his name was chosen or have them brainstorm a list of famous people and characters who share his name. Have each student write his information on provided paper. After every youngster completes his research, sit with students in a circle. Invite each student to tell the class about his name. Your young researchers are sure to agree that names really are special!

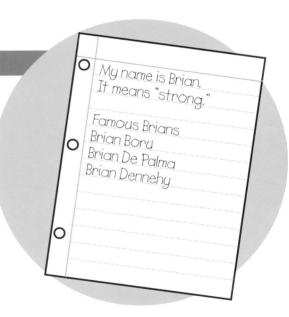

My name is Brian.
It means "strong."

Famous Brians
Brian Boru
Brian De Palma
Brian Dennehy

Great Glyphs

These one-of-a-kind projects reveal a lot about students! Make a copy of the glyph code on page 53 for each student. Place the copies, tape, scissors, and one or more sets of letter stencils at a center that is stocked with pencils and crayons. Also provide a supply of white paper strips that are sized to accommodate the stencils. A student follows the directions to complete his page. Next, he traces letter stencils to spell his name on a paper strip (or two strips taped together). He trims any excess length. Then he decorates his name by the code, using desired colors for the indicated patterns. If a student has more than eight letters in his name, have him color the ninth letter like the first one, the tenth letter like the second one, and so on.

After a student completes his glyph, set aside time for him to show it to the class. Challenge his classmates to interpret his glyph and invite them to ask follow-up questions. Then laminate the glyph and have the youngster tape it to his desk to create a unique (and informative!) nametag.

Did you enjoy this getting-acquainted reproducible? See pages 54 and 55 for more!

Blue-Ribbon Buses

Look who's in the driver's seat! For this back-to-school idea, make a pattern of a bus with several windows. Then give each student a yellow construction paper copy of the pattern. Instruct each student to glue a small photo of herself in the driver's seat and then provide information about herself in each window. Ask each student to cut out her bus and share her busload of information with the class before you post the projects around the room. Students will be ready to roll into a new school year with these clever introductions to their classmates.

Gina Parisi—Grs. 1–6 Basic Skills
Brookdale School
Bloomfield, NJ

C an do math well

H as a good time in art

R eads mysteries

I s excited about third grade

S tudies for every test

One-of-a-Kind Bookmarks

Promote individuality *and* reading with this getting-acquainted project. To make a bookmark, a child writes her name (in all capital letters) vertically along the left edge of a 4½" x 12" strip of construction paper. Next, she writes a self-describing acrostic poem and trims the paper as desired. Collect the bookmarks, laminate them for durability, and then redistribute them, making sure no child receives her own. In turn, each student reads aloud the name on the bookmark she holds. When this classmate stands, she introduces him by reading the acrostic poem he wrote. After the projects are returned to the students who made them, invite each child to hole-punch the top of her bookmark and tie a length of yarn through the hole. Now that's a bookmark that's ready to be used!

Pam Zettervall—Gr. 3
Willard Model Elementary
Norfolk, VA

Math by Any Other Name

Here's a letter-perfect idea for sharpening a variety of math skills while learning classmates' names! Have each student write her first name on a large sticky note. Then help students use the sticky notes to create a graph of name lengths on the chalkboard. Next, orally provide grade-appropriate questions about the graph, such as "What names have more than five letters?" or "What three names have a total of 14 letters?" Ask volunteers to tell the class their answers and write any corresponding number sentences on the chalkboard. Now that's math practice you can count on!

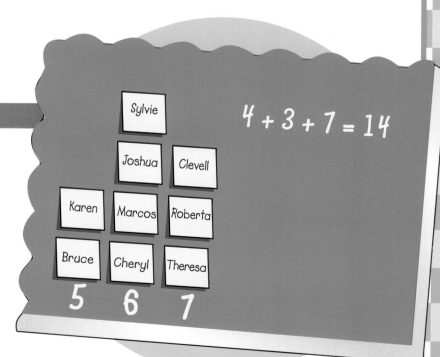

$4 + 3 + 7 = 14$

Sylvie	
Joshua	Clevell
Karen	Marcos	Roberta
Bruce	Cheryl	Theresa

5   6   7

Me

Please help me decide
What item goes inside,
Something about me
So all my friends can see
What I like or do
That makes me special too!

Me Bags

Build self-esteem and help students get to know each other better with this back-to-school activity! For each student, glue to the front of a paper bag a poem like the one shown. Have each child take his bag home and return it on a designated day with an item inside that represents something special about himself. Ask each child to share his item with the class and answer questions from his classmates.

Catherine Salvini—Multiage Grs. 1–2
Morningside Community School
Pittsfield, MA

A Word Search Welcome

Here's a first-day activity that's sure to please! Prepare a word-search puzzle and a corresponding word bank that includes each child's name and your name. After students complete the activity, ask each child to introduce himself to the class and then reveal where in the puzzle his name is located. Send the papers home with students at the end of the day so they can share with their families the names of their new classmates and teacher!

Nell Roberts
The Covenant School
Charlottesville, VA

Making Friends

Foster friendships with this first-day activity. To begin, ask students what they can learn about their teacher by just looking (hair color, height, and so on). Then reveal several things about yourself that cannot be seen, like a favorite place to visit, favorite hobbies and foods, something that scares you, and so on. Help students understand that in order to make a friend it is important to learn things that cannot be seen. Then, on provided paper, have each child write his name and illustrate himself doing something that he enjoys. Hole-punch the pages and compile them in a decorated binder labeled "Making Friends." Encourage students to look at the volume to find classmates who share their interests. If desired, also keep a supply of hole-punched paper handy so students can add illustrations to the book throughout the year.

Betsy Meyer—Gr. 2
Hugh Cassell Elementary
Waynesboro, VA

Classmate Puzzles

What's in the cards? A get-acquainted learning center! Each student cuts a blank 4" x 6" card jigsaw-style to make a two-piece puzzle. She assembles the puzzle and marks each piece to indicate the top. On one half, she writes her name and illustrates a self-portrait. On the other half, she writes a sentence about herself. Store students' prepared puzzle pieces in a gift bag at a center. A student assembles the puzzles to learn about her classmates!

adapted from an idea by Catherine Broome
Melbourne Beach, FL

First-Day Introductions

No doubt youngsters will arrive on the first day of school with plenty of questions about you and their new classmates. Get introductions rolling and set minds at ease with *The Teacher From the Black Lagoon* by Mike Thaler and this activity. To prepare, cover an empty cube-shaped box with colorful paper. Label each side with a different topic, such as hobbies or favorite food. For younger students, add a corresponding picture for each topic.

Inform students that in *The Teacher From the Black Lagoon,* a young boy named Hubie has so many questions about his new teacher that he imagines all kinds of frightful things about her. At this point, poll the students to find out how many of them have questions about you! Then read aloud this amusing book about first-day jitters. At the book's conclusion, gather students in a circle on the floor. Tell them that instead of having their imaginations get the best of them (like Hubie!), you've planned an activity that will help them get to know you, and each other, better. Then roll the prepared cube and respond to the topic that you roll. Have each student take a turn in a similar manner. Repeat as desired. Conclude the activity with a short question-and-answer session to address any remaining concerns.

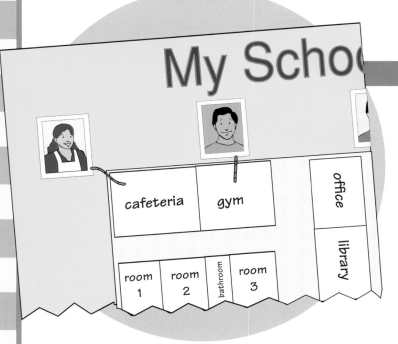

My School

cafeteria | gym | office

room 1 | room 2 | bathroom | room 3 | library

School Map

This first-day activity familiarizes students with their school and staff, and it shows them that a map represents a real place! Ask students to name important places around the school; then post a simple map of the school on a bulletin board. Next, take the class on a walking tour of the school. Be sure to visit each important place, meet the staff members working there, and take an instant picture. When the tour is over, enlist your students' help in mounting the pictures around the edge of the school map and using lengths of yarn to connect the photos to their corresponding map locations.

Jennifer Alexander—Gr. 2
Stocks Elementary
Greenville, NC

Building Self-Esteem

Help your principal get acquainted with your students for all the right reasons! To prepare, you will need the approval of your school principal and a supply of stickers (computer generated or specially ordered) similar to the one shown. When a student demonstrates exemplary behavior or academic success, press a sticker on her clothing and send her to see the principal. The principal then spends a few moments speaking with the child about her success. When the student returns to the classroom, she'll be grinning from ear to ear!

Roxanne Ward—Gr. 3
Greenwood Elementary School
Sylvania, OH

I visited the principal! Ask me about it!

Name_____

GLYPH CODE

Read each box.
Circle the answer.
Follow your teacher's directions to make a glyph.

First Letter
Are you a boy or girl?

boy = ▨

girl = ▦

Second Letter
Do you have any brothers or sisters?

yes = red

no = green

Third Letter
Do you have a pet?

yes = ⬚

no = ⬚

Fourth Letter
Which subject do you like the most?

reading = red
math = blue
science = green
social studies = purple
art = orange
music = yellow
other = brown

Fifth Letter
How do you get to school?

walk = yellow
bus = purple
car = red
van = orange
other = green

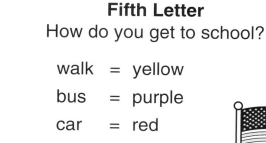

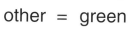

Sixth Letter
Do you like ice cream?

yes = ⬚

no = ⬚

Seventh Letter
Do you like sports?

yes = ⬚

no = ⬚

Eighth Letter
Have you ever been to the beach?

yes = blue

no = orange

Note to the teacher: Use with "Great Glyphs" on page 48.

Players: X = _____   O = _____

Take Your Pick!

To play each game:

1. Choose a partner.
2. Decide who will play first.
3. In turn, pick a square on the gameboard. Share the information about yourself.
4. Draw your symbol in the square.
5. The first player to get three in a row wins!

Game A

favorite food	birthdate	best summer vacation
best friend	number of family members	favorite book
favorite color	favorite hobby	best time in school

Game B

favorite game	number of pets	chores at home
favorite author	goals for the school year	best field trip
favorite place to visit	best school subject	least favorite thing to do

Game C

favorite book character	age	name of a friend
number of times on an airplane	best time on the playground	favorite movie
favorite toy	favorite sport	places lived

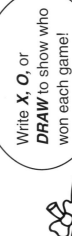

Write *X*, *O*, or *DRAW* to show who won each game!

Game Winners

Game A _____

Game B _____

Game C _____

Bonus Box: On the back of this sheet, make a list of five things you and your partner have in common.

54

©The Mailbox® • *Back-to-School* • TEC1498

A Bushel of Fun

Read the activity on each apple.
Color the apple red if it is something you enjoy.
Color the other apples green.

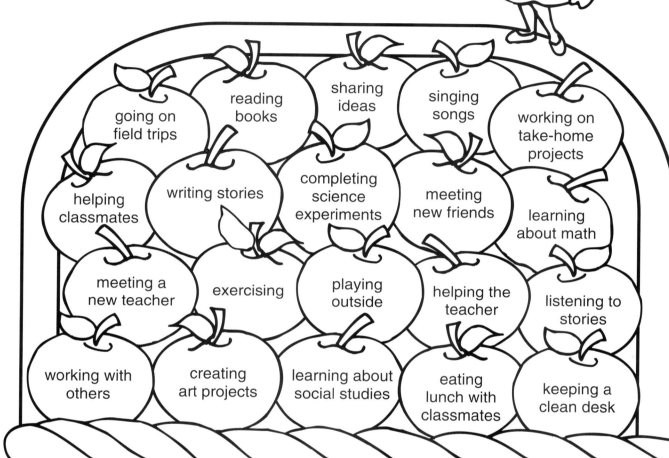

going on field trips

reading books

sharing ideas

singing songs

working on take-home projects

helping classmates

writing stories

completing science experiments

meeting new friends

learning about math

meeting a new teacher

exercising

playing outside

helping the teacher

listening to stories

working with others

creating art projects

learning about social studies

eating lunch with classmates

keeping a clean desk

Complete each sentence.

1. The best thing about school is _____
_____.

2. I am really good at _____
_____.

3. This year I really want to learn _____
_____.

Bonus Box: On the back of this sheet, write three ways you think this school year will be different from last year.

Picture-Perfect Birthdays

Student photographs make this monthly display a kid-pleasing favorite! To prepare, take and develop a photograph of each student. Label the back of each photograph with the child's birthdate. (If the child has a summer birthday, also write the date of his half birthday and plan to recognize him in the corresponding month.) Store the photographs in envelopes by month for easy retrieval. Divide a poster-size tagboard rectangle as shown. Add a title and decorations; then laminate it. Display the resulting poster in a prominent classroom location.

At the beginning of each month, use a wipe-off marker to program the poster. Add the photographs of the students who celebrate birthdays that month and label each photograph with the appropriate date. Direct students' attention to the display and lead the class in a birthday song for the honored youngsters. At the end of the month, remove the photographs and present them to the appropriate students.

Pat Rigueira—Gr. 3
Southern Cross School
Buenos Aires, Argentina

A Festive Display

Brighten your classroom with a year-round birthday reference! For each month, place a stick-on bow at the top of a vertically positioned 9" x 12" sheet of construction paper. Title the paper with the month. Write the name of each student who has a birthday in that month and the corresponding date. Mount the posters in order along a classroom wall, alternating them with noisemakers. Title the display "Birthday Celebrations Are in Order!"

Katie Robinson—Gr. 3
Limestone Walters School
Peoria, IL

September
Scott: 16
Debbie: 26

Animal Crackers

Special Treats

Here's a tempting birthday suggestion! Obtain a variety of individually wrapped snacks. Decorate each one with a bow. Place the snacks in a basket along with birthday-themed books. On a youngster's special day, ask her to choose a treat and a book to enjoy during snacktime. Replenish the supply of snacks as necessary throughout the year. Now that's a birthday idea sure to take the cake!

adapted from an idea by Linda Clark—Gr. 2
Carlisle Public School
Carlisle, MA

Make a Wish!

Spread birthday cheer with a class book! To keep the details of the book a surprise for the birthday child, have the youngster visit the school library or another suitable location while the rest of the class prepares the book. Invite students to brainstorm things the birthday child likes. Then give each student a copy of the form on page 59.

The student writes the birthday child's name where indicated and writes a wish that reflects the child's interests. She illustrates her work in the provided space, colors the rest of the form as desired, and signs her name on the gift tag. She glues the completed form onto a 6" x 9" piece of construction paper. Collect the resulting pages and bind them between construction paper covers. After the birthday child returns to the classroom, present him with the book of wishes. What a thoughtful gift!

Michele Culver—Gr. 2
Altamonte Elementary School
Altamonte Springs, FL

Greetings Galore

No doubt this oversized greeting card will delight its recipient! A day or two before a student's birthday, fold an 18" x 24" piece of white bulletin board paper in half to make a card. Place the card in a center stocked with crayons and markers. For message-writing inspiration, provide a list of student-generated birthday greetings or a supply of recycled birthday cards. Arrange for each child to visit the center. Have him copy a greeting, write an original message, or draw an illustration on the card. Then ask him to sign his name. Invite a student volunteer to decorate the front of the card to complete this memorable keepsake.

adapted from an idea by Gina Reagan—Gr. 3
Summerfield Elementary
Summerfield, NC

Guests of Honor

What's on the menu? Monthly birthday celebrations! Designate one day each month for lunch with birthday students and one day at the end of the year for lunch with students who have summer birthdays. Distribute invitations to the honored youngsters (see "You're Invited!" on this page). Arrange to eat with your guests at a cafeteria or classroom table that you have decorated for the occasion. If desired, bring in cupcakes for a special dessert. During lunch invite each student to talk about her special day!

Jennifer Farrand
St. Thomas the Apostle School
West Hartford, CT

You're Invited!

If you eat lunch with students on their birthdays, this reproducible invitation will come in handy. Prepare a copy of the invitation on page 59 for each lunch guest. Fold it, label the outside with the name of the intended recipient, and add a birthday sticker to prepare it for delivery.

Linnae Nicholas—Gr. 2
Cuba Elementary School
Cuba, NY

Jan.						
Feb.						
Mar.						
Apr.						
May						
June						
July						
Aug.						
Sept.						
Oct.						
Nov.						
Dec.						

Birthday Graph

Here's a first-day activity that teaches and pleases students! Display a large bar graph titled "Birthday Graph." With your students' help, list the 12 months of the year on the graph. Next, have each child write her name and birthdate on the graph for the correct month and lightly color the corresponding square. Pose questions about the completed graph for students to answer. Then, after a review of monthly abbreviations, have each child label a 9" x 12" sheet of one-inch graph paper to make a birthday graph and then color the spaces to correspond to the posted graph. Students will be proud to share these first-day projects with their families, and you'll feel good about the concepts you've covered!

Pamela Williams—Gr. 3
Dixieland Elementary
Lakeland, FL

Happy Birthday Journal

This journal-writing activity is the icing on the cake! Prepare a cake-shaped writing journal. On the first page, write and illustrate a short story that describes your most recent birthday. Then place the journal, a pack of crayons, and a sharpened birthday pencil in a birthday gift bag. Each child takes the bag home on or near his birthday and completes a journal page about his birthday celebration. (Establish a plan for celebrating summer birthdays throughout the year.) When he returns the bag, ask him to share his entry with the class. Happy birthday!

Beverley Price
Pinar Elementary
Orlando, FL

Handcrafted Birthday Cards

Here's a birthday card project that really takes the cake! Each child folds a 12" x 18" sheet of white construction paper in half and writes on the back of the card "Made just for you by [student's name]." Then she decorates the front of the card, making the most spectacular birthday card she's ever seen. Collect the cards and inside each one write "Happy Birthday From the Whole Gang!" To recognize a child's birthday, select a card he did not make and ask each of his classmates to sign it. Ask the classmate who designed the card to present it to the birthday student. Be sure to establish a plan for celebrating summer birthdays throughout the year!

Suzie Robinson
Pioneer Elementary School
Neoga, IL

Happy Birthday,

_____!

Here is my birthday wish for you:

From:

Birthday Celebration

Dear _____,

It's time to celebrate your birthday!
You're invited to join me for lunch on

_____.

You may bring a bag lunch or purchase
one from the cafeteria.

Sincerely,

_____

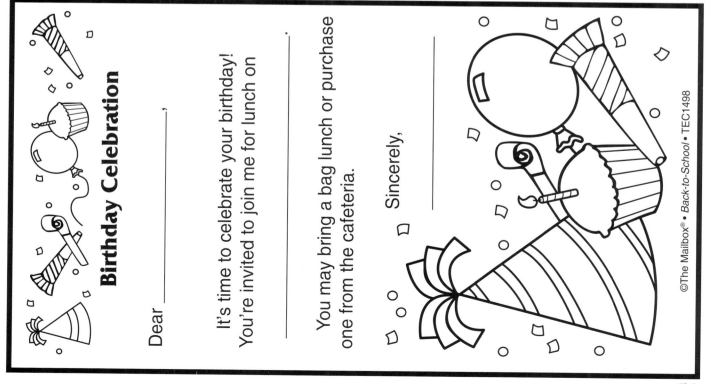

Communication Binder

Keeping track of parent communication just got easier! Prepare a communication form similar to the one shown. For each student, program a copy of the form and label a tabbed divider with pockets. Secure the materials in a binder so that each student's form faces the corresponding divider. Store written correspondence in the pocket and jot down notes from phone calls and meetings on the form.

Christie Peiffer
Seabourn Elementary
Mesquite, TX

School Supplies Request

This handy request form encourages student responsibility. First, make several copies of a form similar to the one shown. When a student needs a supply, he fills out a form. After his request is approved by you, he takes the form home. Parents are sure to appreciate this clear and concise method of communication.

Lynn MacLennan
Byers Elementary
Byers, CO

Weekly Quotes

Keep parents informed and entertained with an easy-to-publish weekly edition of classroom news! Near the end of each day, gather student quotes about the day's events and write them on a dated form like the one shown. On Friday add a note from you and then make a copy for each student. Have each child describe or illustrate her favorite event of the week on the newspaper she's taking home. Extra! Extra! Read all about the week!

Christine Schirmer
Van Zant Elementary School
Marlton, NJ

Timesaving Forms

Count on parents to give this communication convenience rave reviews. Prepare a form for each of several common occasions that require a parent note. Duplicate each form on colored paper to make two copies per child. Staple each student's forms into a booklet. Distribute the booklets at open house or send them home with a note of explanation. A parent removes a form from the booklet as needed, completes it, and returns it to school with her child.

Joan Turner—Gr. 2
Oakbrook Elementary
Ladson, SC

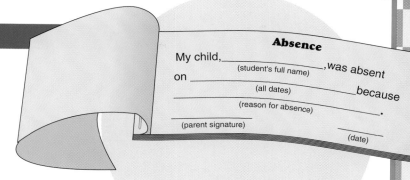

Absence

My child,_____,was absent
(student's full name)
on _____
(all dates)
_____ because
(reason for absence)
_____.
(parent signature)
_____
(date)

Meet the Class

Instead of sending home the interest inventories that your students complete on the first day of school, collect and publish them in a three-ring notebook. For durability, insert the students' papers into plastic page protectors. Also include a photograph of each student with his interest inventory if desired. Then arrange for each child to take home the notebook so he can introduce his family to his new classmates. Each time a new student joins your class, update the notebook and then invite him to take it home for the evening so he can quickly get to know his new classmates!

Lynn Lupo-Hudgins
Austin Road Elementary
Stockbridge, GA

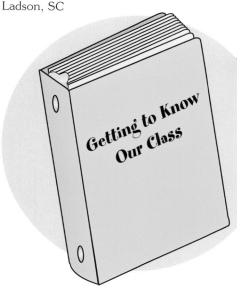

Getting to Know Our Class

Help Wanted

Could you use help with your reading program? This one-of-a-kind parent note is guaranteed to catch the eye of every potential volunteer! Design a help wanted ad that describes your needs (see illustration for clarity). Send home a copy of the ad with every student, and before you know it, you'll have plenty of eager volunteers.

Bonnie Lanterman
Armstrong Elementary School
Hazelwood, MO

HELP WANTED!

Energetic, friendly, and lovable second-grade children seek reliable, kind, and caring people to listen to and help them as they practice reading.

No experience necessary.   All materials provided.

Pay: Many thanks and a great opportunity to see progress in the children's reading.

If interested in this exciting opportunity, circle a time or times below, write your name and phone number, and cut along the dotted line.

Send the completed form to school with your child.

Thank you,

The Second-Grade Teachers

Monday	Tuesday	Wednesday	Thursday	Friday
10:30–11:30	12:30–1:30	10:30–11:30	12:30–1:30	10:30–11:30
12:30–1:30	2:00–2:40	12:30–1:30	2:00–3:00	12:30–1:30
2:00–3:00		2:00–3:00		2:00–3:00

Name_____ Phone _____

Dear Family,

Today I won a spelling bee.

Love,
Kelsie

Parent Pen Pals

Foster positive communication between parent and child with this noteworthy idea! At the beginning of the school year, ask parents to supply several self-addressed, stamped envelopes. Periodically have students write letters to their parents about their accomplishments and upcoming school events. Facilitate responses from parents by providing them with several postcards addressed to the school. Parents will appreciate being kept up-to-date, and students' writing skills will improve as well.

Karen Smith
Pine Lane Elementary Home School
Pace, FL

Student Self-Evaluation

To add student insight to your conferences, have each child complete a report card (or a similar form of self-evaluation) to assess her progress. After you meet with the child to acknowledge her successes and set goals for the future, place her self-evaluation with the materials you'll be sharing with her parent at conference time. When you review an evaluation with a parent, note whether the child has an accurate perception of her strengths and weaknesses. This insight into a child's self-esteem and her feelings about school are of utmost importance when developing a plan for her continued success.

Lisa Strieker—Gr. 3
St. Paul Elementary School
Highland, IL

My Report Card

by ___Teleana___ on ___Nov. 1, 2005___

Subject	Grade	Subject	Grade
reading	B	social studies	B
spelling	D	science	A
writing	D	music	B
math	A+	art	A+

Behavior Comment: I am good most of the time, except when I talk too much.

Goals: I will practice my spelling words. I will write more sentences in my journal.

Dear Tommy,

You are doing great in spelling!

Love,
Mom

A Warm Welcome

These heartfelt greetings are sure to help parents feel right at home in the classroom. Prior to conferences, have each child write and illustrate a card or letter for his parent that welcomes her to the classroom. Collect the cards. Then, as each parent sits down to talk with you, present her with the card her child designed especially for this occasion. When you wrap up the conference, give each parent paper on which to jot her child a note. Ask her to tuck the greeting inside her child's desk as she leaves.

Jeannette Freeman—Primary
San Antonio School
San Juan, Puerto Rico

Organizing Important Letters

Locating important letters and handouts for parents is a breeze with this timesaving idea. Label one pocket folder for each of these topics: beginning of the school year, end of the school year, conferences, articles, report cards, invitations, permission slips, and miscellaneous. Hole-punch the folders and place them in a large, three-ring binder. Keep original copies of letters and handouts for parents in the folders. At the beginning of the month, browse through the folders and duplicate the items you need. Locating needed materials has never been easier!

Linh Tran
Charles B. Wallace Elementary
York, PA

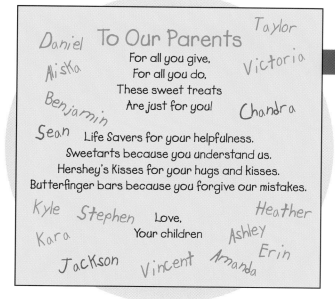

Friendship Basket

Here's a sweet way to connect with parents! Fill a large basket with assorted wrapped candies that include Life Savers, Sweetarts, Hershey's Kisses, and Butterfinger candies. On poster board, write a parent greeting like the one shown. Share the greeting with the class and explain that you will display it and the basket of goodies during conferences. Next, ask each child to sign the poster with a colorful marker and invite him to select one candy from the basket for himself. Display the greeting and goodies near your conference table. Parents are sure to appreciate the sweets as well as the sentiment!

Dee Dee Cooper
Monterey Elementary
Monterey, LA

Student Participation

If your district encourages students to attend parent-teacher conferences, here's an idea you can use! Invite each child to be in charge of the first five minutes of his conference! Suggest that during this time he introduce you to his parent, tell what he especially likes about this school year, and describe the school-related achievement of which he is most proud. During the remainder of the conference, welcome input from both the parent and the child. This approach encourages the child to reflect on his progress and help determine goals for the year. Communication has never been clearer!

Lou Whipple
Holy Cross School
Kansas City, MO

My favorite subject is math because Ms. Lewis makes it fun!

"I Can!" Mobile

Students will be proud to prepare these projects for parent-teacher conferences! First, have each child list on paper five things he can now do that he couldn't do at the end of the previous school year. Next, distribute white construction paper copies of page 65. A child personalizes and colors the large can. He writes the items from his list on the cards, each in a different blank space. Then he adds the date, colors the remaining artwork, and cuts out the five cards and the can. He folds each card along the thin line, keeping the programming to the outside. Then he hole-punches two holes in the large can where indicated and ties a one-yard length of yarn to each hole. One at a time, he slides each folded card onto the bottom yarn length (keeping the yarn sandwiched between the paper) and glues the blank sides together.

As a parent leaves the conference, give him his child's "I Can" mobile and a copy or two of the blank cards from page 65. Suggest that the parent display the mobile in the home and encourage his child to continue adding cards (and yarn as needed) to the project throughout the school year!

adapted from an idea by Georgia Hayes
Christian Center School
Sioux Falls, SD

Voice Mail Communications

If you have a voice mail system at your school, here's a communication tip for you! At the end of each school day, record a new voice mail greeting that highlights the events of that day. Encourage parents to call each day and listen to your message. Parents will appreciate the daily updates and find them useful when talking with their children about their day at school.

Barbara Meland
Mounds Park Elementary
Saint Paul, MN

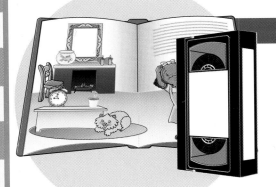

Reading Progress

Impress parents by providing them with up-close and personal accounts of their youngsters' oral reading skills! In advance, videotape each child reading a passage at his current reading level. After a parent views the tape of her child, discuss the specific reading strategies the youngster is using as well as his progress. Then, as appropriate, offer suggestions for strengthening the child's reading skills. Now that's bringing a youngster's reading skills into focus!

Marjorie O'Reilly
Walt Whitman School
Wheeling, IL

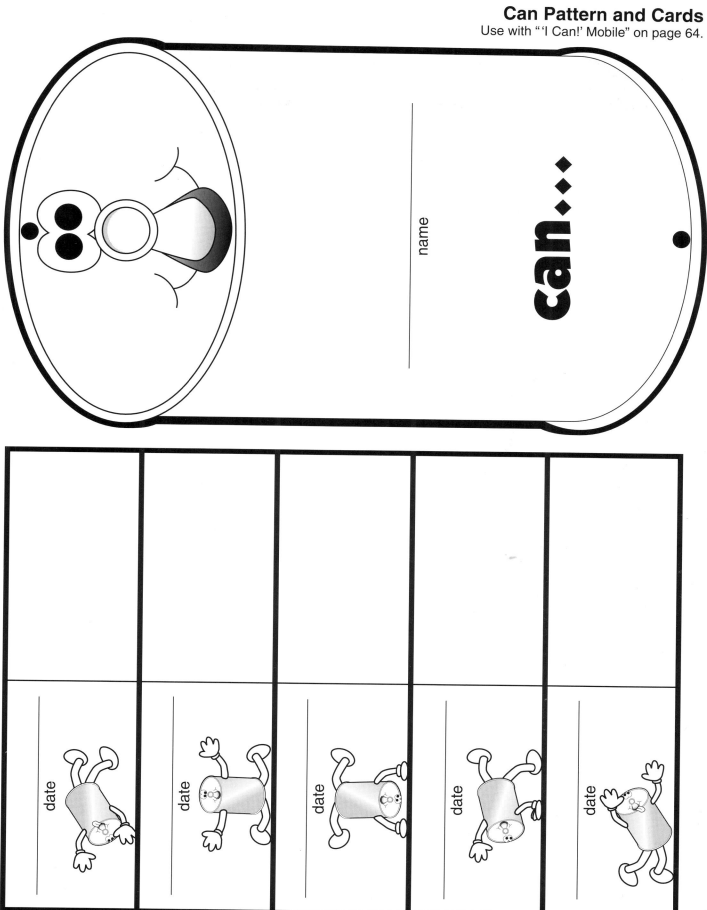

name

can...

date

date

date

date

date

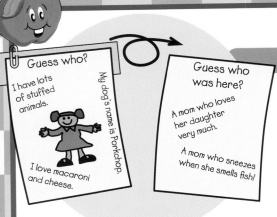

Who Sits Where?

Students provide the clues, and parents solve the case! The day of open house, have each child draw her self-portrait and write a few clues about her identity on drawing paper. Help students paper-clip their projects atop their desktags so that their names are hidden from view. Parents study the projects to determine where their children sit during the day, using the desktags to confirm their hunches. For added fun, invite each parent to turn her child's project over and write a message to her child on the back—using clues, of course!

Valdarine S. Kemp, Oakes Field Primary School
Nassau, Bahamas

The Parent Game

Try this open house icebreaker! On the day of open house, have each student list his favorite food, book, color, song, and place to visit on provided paper. Then, at open house, have each parent list the same information about his child. Invite parents to predict how well they think they've done on this little pop quiz; then have them compare their answers with the responses their children gave earlier in the day. Parents are sure to enjoy the activity, and you'll have quickly put the group at ease.

Joyce Sutherland, Pecan Grove Elementary
Richmond, TX

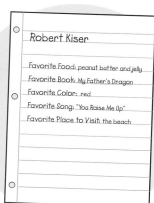

Slide Show Extravaganza

Most parents would love to know what happens during a typical school day, so why not show them! Photograph students involved in daily activities, making sure that every child is caught on film. Then sequence the slides so that a typical school day unfolds. Preview the slide show with your youngsters and, if desired, write a class-created script for the production. You may not win an award for your efforts, but you'll definitely receive plenty of praise from pleased parents!

Lori Demlow—Gr. 2, Heritage Lakes
Glendale Heights, IL

Picture-Perfect Parade

These unique get-acquainted projects make an irresistible open house display! Ask each student to bring photographs from home that show him and various family members engaged in assorted activities. Or have students illustrate similar scenes on photo-size rectangles of drawing paper. Then have each child create a full-body self-portrait, like the one shown, on which to exhibit his pictures. Ask older students to pen captions for their pictures too. After each child presents his project to the class, display it in the hallway outside your classroom door. The result is a picture-perfect parade that's guaranteed to stop open house visitors in their tracks!

Katie Robinson—Gr. 3, Limestone Walters School
Peoria, IL

Graph It!

It's easy to create a kid-pleasing graphing lesson during open house! Make two identical "Choose Your Favorite" bar graphs like the one shown. The day of open house, have each child write his name on a sticky note and attach it to one graph. As parents enter the classroom that evening for open house, ask them to write their names on individual sticky notes and attach the notes to the second graph. Parents are sure to find the graphs interesting, and students will have a ball evaluating and comparing them the following day!

Charlene Afflitto—Gr. 2, Grandview School
North Caldwell, NJ

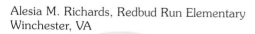

Choose Your Favorite Fast Food												
Burger												
Hot dog												
Pizza												
Taco												
Other												

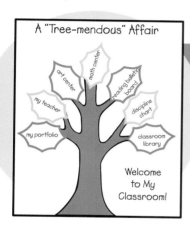

A "Tree-mendous" Affair

art center
math center
reading bulletin board
my teacher
discipline chart
my portfolio
classroom library

Welcome to My Classroom!

A "Tree-mendous" Affair

You can count on plenty of enthusiasm when you ask students to be open house tour guides! To prepare, make a pattern of a tree with leaves and label it (as shown). Make a white construction paper copy for each child. Talk with the class about the role of a tour guide and write a student-generated list of open house attractions on the chalkboard. Then give each child a copy of the tree and have her write a favorite attraction on each leaf. Invite each student to color her itinerary; then have her place it on her desktop to use for open house that evening. Parents are sure to enjoy and benefit from the guided tour, students will feel "tree-mendous" about their participation, and you'll be thankful for the time you spent visiting with your guests.

Cathy Howlett—Gr. 3, Franklin Elementary
Mt. Airy, NC

Family Puzzles

They're not exactly door prizes, but they could be the next best thing for promoting open house participation! On the day of open house, have each child illustrate his family on provided paper. Then have him cut his artwork into a designated number of pieces and store the pieces in a personalized envelope or zippered bag on his desktop. When parents arrive, they'll be eager to piece together the puzzles their children have prepared for them. And you can anticipate plenty of smiles as the family portraits take shape!

Alesia M. Richards, Redbud Run Elementary
Winchester, VA

Each afternoon we have Buddy Reading. We take turns reading to a friend.

Just Hangin' Out!

Give your guests a clear picture of day-to-day activities at this eye-catching display. Photograph each child engaged in a different school-related activity; then mount each snapshot on a T-shirt cutout. Ask each child to write on her cutout a caption that describes what she is doing in the photograph. Title a bulletin board "Hangin' Out in [grade level]!" and use lengths of heavy string or plastic clothesline and clothespins to suspend the projects.

Sandy Preston—Gr. 2, North Street Elementary
Brockway, PA

An apple for the teacher
Is really nothing new,
Except when you remember
Parents are teachers too!

Open House Apples

Apples are for teachers, right? So what could be more appropriate than presenting your students' parents with apples at open house? To prepare each apple, wrap it in plastic wrap and then use a length of curling ribbon to secure the wrap at the top. Write the poem shown on a leaf cutout. Hole-punch the leaf, thread the curling ribbon through the hole, and tie the ribbon ends. What a great way to let parents know how much their involvement is appreciated and needed!

Jo Fryer, Kildeer Countryside School
Long Grove, IL

Customizing Your Raffle

Everyone knows that a raffle is a great way to boost open house attendance. But did you ever consider that a raffle is also a great opportunity to gather information? To customize your raffle, create a raffle ticket that gives parents an opportunity to ask questions (like the one shown) or elicits information from them (such as special interests and skills). Encourage each family attending open house to fill out one raffle ticket. Hold the raffle the following day and award the winner the promised prize. Then read the raffle tickets to follow up on the information you've gathered.

M. J. Owen—Gr. 3, Baty Elementary
Del Valle, TX

Open House Raffle

Parent's name _____
Child's name _____
Questions I have: _____
_____
_____

The Secret's Out!

We had a multiplication bee today and I won!

Parents will be as pleased as punch to learn that the typical response to "What did you do at school today?" should no longer be "Nothing!" During open house, inform parents that you conclude each school day by reviewing the events of that day. This means that with a bit of encouragement every child will have something to share about his day!

Kate Pointkowski—Gr. 2, Spring Hill Elementary School
McLean, VA

One-of-a-Kind Presentation

Patterning your open house presentation after a popular game show is sure to bring rave reviews from parents. To play a game similar to the Jeopardy game, create a gameboard by taping construction paper squares labeled with dollar amounts to the chalkboard as shown; then write a different school-related category above each column. To play, parents take turns picking categories and dollar amounts. After each selection is made, announce an answer related to the chosen category and challenge the group to furnish the corresponding question. Keep the game moving right along by giving extra clues when needed. Parents will appreciate your efforts to entertain and enlighten them!

Classroom Rules	School Staff	Curriculum	Special Celebrations	Misc.
$5	$5	$5	$5	$5
$10	$10	$10	$10	$10
$15	$15	$15	$15	$15
$20	$20	$20	$20	$20
$25	$25	$25	$25	$25

Jeannie Frye—Gr. 3, Alvord Elementary
Alvord, TX

Superstar Students

Propel your youngsters' self-esteems to extraordinary heights with these parent-authored stories. Make and personalize a superstar form similar to the one shown for each child. Send each child's form home with a visiting parent or send it home with the child on the day following open house. A parent describes her child's superstar status, signs and dates the form, and then returns it to school by a designated date. With lots of fanfare, read aloud the parent projects for all the children to enjoy. If desired, laminate the keepsake projects before presenting them to the students.

Diane Outlaw
San Antonio, TX

Child-Centered Survey

Open the door to valuable information when you invite parents to share insights and information about their children. Place a copy of the survey on page 71 on each child's desk and request that parents complete the form during their open house visit. As you collect the surveys, assure parents that you will promptly follow up on any concerns that they have. Label the remaining surveys with the appropriate student names and send them home the following day for parents to fill out and return. In just one evening you'll have sent a clear message that you value and encourage input from parents. And you'll have learned a lot too!

Ritsa Tassopoulos—Gr. 3, Oakdale Elementary
Cincinnati, OH

High Five Banner

When students lay their eyes on this colorful banner the day following open house, they'll grin from ear to ear! During open house, ask each visitor to add his handprint and an encouraging message to a length of white bulletin board paper that you've provided for this purpose. (To make a handprint, a parent paints colorful tempera paint on his hand before he presses it on the paper.) Display the parent-made project in a prominent classroom location all year long. It will be a great source of motivation for all!

adapted from an idea by Becky Hilbrands—Gr. 3, Remsen-Union Elementary
Remsen, IA

Phone Home

Keep an open line of communication between school and home by announcing a phone home plan during open house. Whether you agree to phone home once a month or once a week, parents will be pleased to know that you'll be checking in and giving them an opportunity to express their satisfaction and concerns. Brrring!

Rebecca Abney Roy—Grs. 2–3, Centerfield Elementary
Oldham County, KY

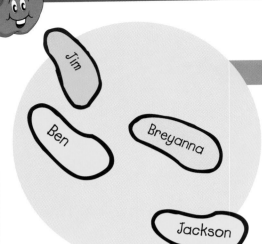

Follow the Footprints

Let colorful footprints guide your open house visitors right to your classroom door! Have each child trace the shape of each of his feet onto colorful paper and then cut out and personalize each resulting footprint. Use the cutouts to create a path from the front doors of the school to your classroom door!

Fran Blaess
Middletown, RI

Remember When...

Parents are sure to enjoy taking a trip down memory lane! Ask each parent to copy the story starter "When I was in [child's grade level]…" on a sheet of paper and complete it by writing about a memorable experience from that grade. Provide crayons for illustrations. Collect the projects at the end of the evening. Over the next several days, share a handful of the stories with your youngsters during storytime. When all the stories have been read, bind them and give each child an opportunity to take the collection home to share with his family.

Del Bull, Jesse Boyd Elementary
Spartanburg, SC

Making Party Plans

The evening of open house is the perfect time to round up donations for upcoming classroom parties. Create a sign-up sheet, like the one shown, for each party. Post the sheets in a prominent classroom location and encourage parents to sign up throughout the evening. As each scheduled party draws near, confirm donations by contacting the parents on the corresponding list. Easy as pie!

Roxanne Ward, Greenwood Elementary School
Sylvania, OH

Recruiting Volunteers

Open house is also the perfect time to recruit parent volunteers. During your presentation, briefly inform parents of your needs and direct them to an area of the classroom where you've posted colorful sign-up sheets that clearly outline a variety of ways in which they can help—at school and from home. Then stand back and watch in amazement as signatures begin to accumulate!

Rebecca Abney Roy, Centerfield Elementary
Oldham County, KY

Tell Me About Your Child

My child's name is _____.

My child's interests and/or hobbies include _____
_____.

My child's favorite subject is _____
_____.

My child's special qualities include _____
_____.

My child approaches learning

_____with excitement   _____with curiosity

_____with confidence   _____with anxiety

_____with reluctance   _____without interest

Goals for my child include _____
_____
_____
_____.

Questions or concerns that I have: _____
_____
_____
_____.

This survey will be strictly confidential. Thank you for helping make this a great year for your child.

Note to the teacher: Use with "Child-Centered Survey" on page 69.

71

"Apple-tizing" Prints

Students can use this fun printing technique to decorate a bushel of school-related items like folders, nametags, notebooks, and more! Pour red and green tempera paints into individual shallow containers. Place the item to be decorated on a flat, newspaper-covered surface. To make an apple print, dip one end of a large marshmallow into the red paint and then press it onto the item. To make an apple leaf, insert a toothpick into one end of a small marshmallow (for a handle), dip the small marshmallow into the green paint, and press it near the top of the apple print. When the paint is dry, use a black permanent marker to draw desired stems. "Apple-lutely" scrumptious!

Elizabeth Searls Almy
Greensboro, NC

Personality Plus

Not only are these projects packed with personality, but they also reveal something about students' family members and pets!

1. Give each child a large T-shirt shape cut from a 9" x 12" sheet of construction paper. Ask that he take the shirt cutout home, decorate it with drawings or pictures of family members and pets, and return the cutout to school.
2. When all the cutouts have been returned, have each student paint a 12" x 18" sheet of art paper with a skin-toned paint that approximates his own coloring.
3. When the painted paper has dried, have the student draw two arm outlines and a head-and-neck outline on his paper and cut them out.
4. Have each student glue the arm and head cutouts onto his T-shirt cutout.
5. Encourage each student to cut out and decorate a construction paper hat of his own design and then glue it on the head cutout.
6. Have each student use colorful markers to draw facial features.
7. To complete the effect, have students glue on paper and yarn to represent hair and accessories.

Ellen M. Stern
Alberta Smith Elementary
Midlothian, VA

Schoolwork Frames

Students and parents will agree that these fabulous frames are perfect for displaying schoolwork. Glue the ends of four poster board strips (two 2" x 12" strips and two 2" x 14" strips) together to create a rectangle. When the resulting frame is dry, decorate it with stickers, construction paper scraps and glue, and/or markers. Next, turn the frame over and center a gallon-size resealable plastic bag over the opening. Securely tape the bottom and sides of the bag to the frame. Then open the bag, carefully insert the end of a stapler, and staple the bag (just below the zipper) to the frame. Lastly, press lengths of half-inch self-adhesive magnetic tape around the perimeter of the back of the project. A student slips a work sample into his frame and then proudly displays his project on his family's refrigerator. Encourage students to replace their samples one or more times a week!

Elizabeth Searls Almy
Greensboro, NC

Sunny Pencil Boxes

Spread some sunshine and minimize messy desks with these eye-catching pencil holders!

Materials for one pencil box:
the bottom 2½" of a cereal box
strips of green poster board, 2½" wide
   (to cover the sides of the precut box)
7" yellow construction paper semicircle
2½" x 6" strip of yellow construction paper
1½" x 5" strip of construction paper
construction paper scraps
crayons or markers
glue
scissors

Steps:
1. Glue the green poster board strips to the four sides of the precut cereal box.
2. Cut out facial features from the construction paper scraps and glue them to the semicircle to make a cute sun character.
3. Glue the sun inside the back panel of the holder.
4. Cut the strip of yellow paper into short lengths. Glue the resulting sun rays around the edge of the sun.
5. Personalize the remaining construction paper strip and glue it to the front panel of the holder.

Elizabeth Searls Almy

"Thumb" Apples!

These apple trees are truly "thumb-thing" special! To begin, tear a tree trunk shape from brown paper and glue it on a 9" x 12" sheet of white construction paper. Use green tempera paint and a sponge to paint the tree's foliage. When the green paint is dry, pour a mixture of liquid soap and red tempera paint into a shallow pan. Use the paint to make a desired number of red thumbprint apples on and near the tree. Allow time for the paint to dry. Then use crayons or markers to add colorful details and a background scene that would make Johnny Appleseed proud!

adapted from an idea by Jane Manuel
Wellington, TX

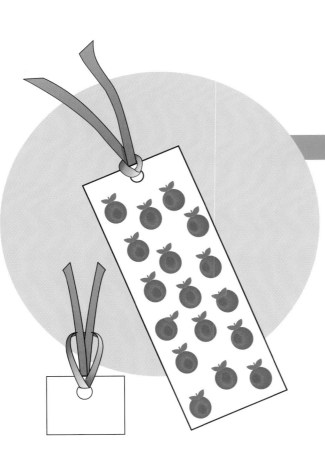

Back-to-School Bookmark

This decorative bookmark is sure to promote a bushel of reading! To make a bookmark, use red paint to make a number of thumbprints on a 2" x 6" piece of white tagboard. Allow the paint to dry. Then, with the project vertically positioned, use a marker to add leaves and stems to the prints so that they resemble apples. Hole-punch the top of the project. Next, fold a 12-inch length of ribbon in half. Push the folded end through the hole, poke the ribbon ends through the resulting loop, and then gently pull the ends snug to make a tassel. There you have it—a handy bookmark just in time for National Library Card Sign-Up Month!

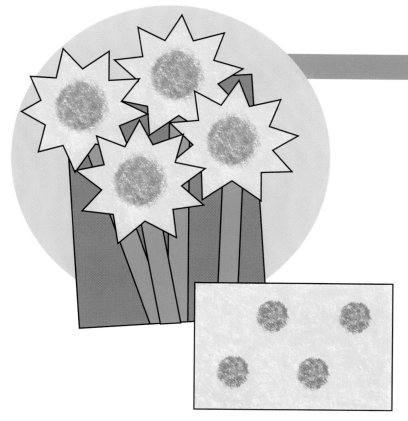

Sunflower Patch

Unlike real sunflowers, these sponge-painted replicas cannot turn their heads toward the sun. However, they are capable of turning the heads of passersby! To begin, dip a damp sponge piece into a shallow container of brown paint. Repeatedly press the sponge (reloading it as needed) onto a 12" x 18" sheet of white art paper to make four large, evenly spaced sunflower centers. Allow the paint to dry; then use yellow paint and a second piece of sponge to paint the remainder of the paper. When dry, cut a sun shape around each sunflower center. Glue a 1" x 12" green paper stem to the back of each flower and then arrange the sunflowers on a 9" x 12" sheet of blue paper. Glue each stem and flower center to the paper. Trim off overhanging stems and display the sunny flowers for all to see!

Me Monuments

With a pinch here and a pat there, students can create monuments spotlighting themselves. Give each child a sheet of waxed paper and two golf ball–sized portions of Crayola Model Magic modeling compound. Or prepare your favorite paintable, air-drying dough recipe. Working atop his waxed paper, a child forms a shape from one ball of dough that represents a favorite interest or hobby. With the remaining ball of dough, he forms a base for his shape. Then he molds the shape to the base. When his resulting monument is dry, he paints it as desired. Lastly, he folds an index card in half and writes his name and a description of his monument on the front. Group your students' monuments and description cards together for a display that's sure to attract plenty of attention during open house!

Kathy Moore—Gr. 3
Stone Creek Elementary School
Rockford, IL

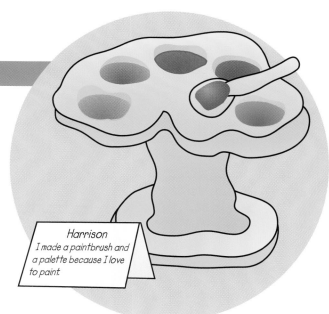

Harrison
I made a paintbrush and a palette because I love to paint.

Welcome Back!

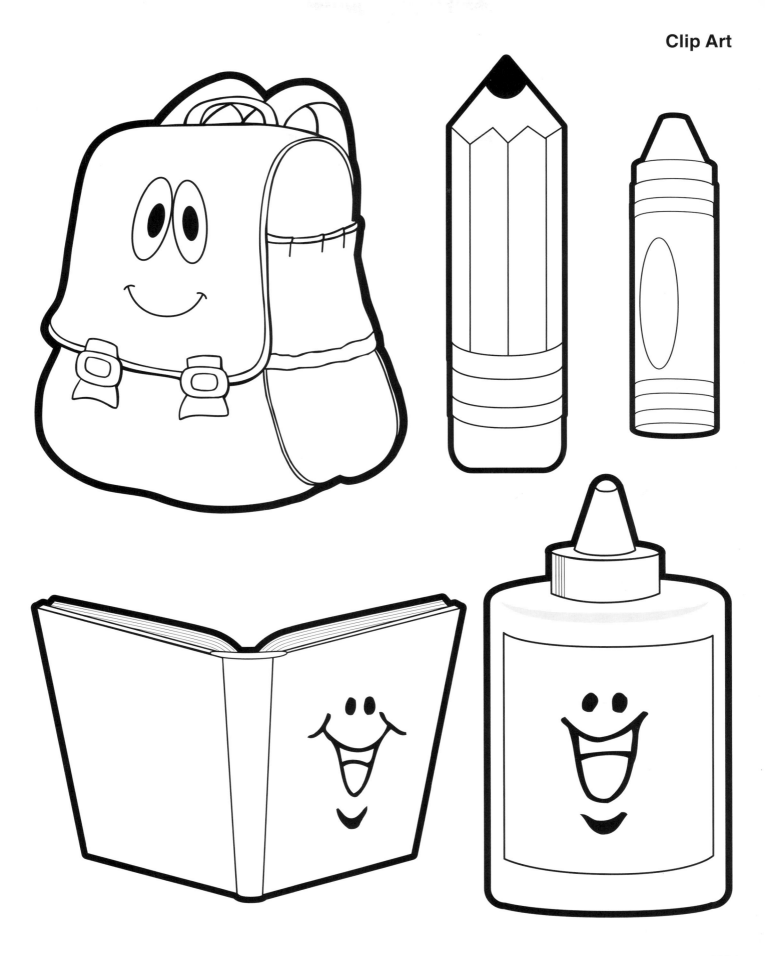

The Spotlight's on Me!

Write nouns and adjectives to complete the lists below.

Nouns That Name Me

Adjectives That Describe Me

Now write a paragraph that describes you.
Include some words from above in your paragraph.

Getting to Know

_____
name

Words About Me

"No-body" Like Me

Draw a picture of yourself in the box below.

Draw a picture of your favorite animal in the box below.

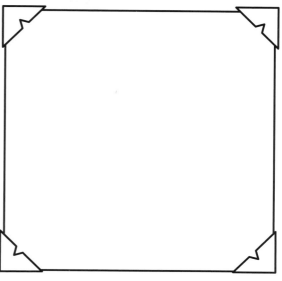

Now compare the two pictures to complete the Venn diagram. Write at least five facts in each area of the diagram.

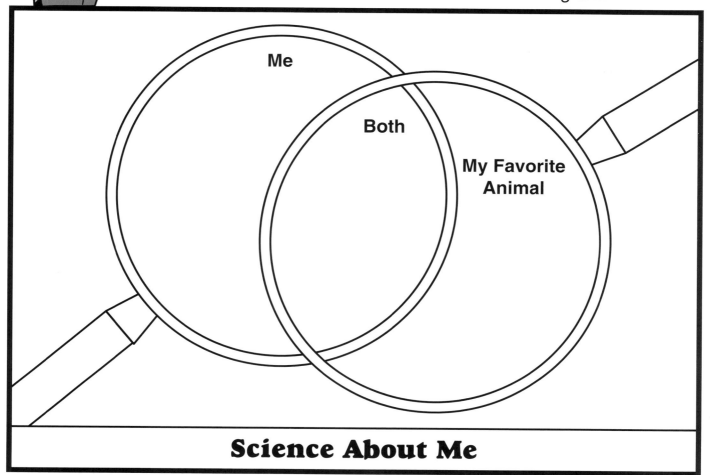

Me

Both

My Favorite Animal

Science About Me

Me and My World

Complete the sentences in each box.
Then draw and color a matching illustration.

The city or town I live in is _____. I like my city or town because _____.	The state or province I live in is _____. I like my state or province because _____.
The country I live in is _____. I like my country because _____.	The continent I live on is _____. I like my continent because _____.

Social Studies About Me

Name _____

It's Pickin' Time!

Add a period or a question mark to the end of each sentence.
Then use the code to color each apple.

1. Let's pick the apples

2. Where are the apples

3. The apples are in the trees

4. How many apples should we pick

5. Pick all of the ripe apples

6. Take the apples to the market

7. Who will buy the apples

8. People buy apples

9. What are apples used for

10. Apples can be used to make pies

11. Apples can be used to make cider

12. Apples are a healthy snack

Color Code

. = red
? = green

Now write the number for each red apple below.

____ ____ ____

____ ____ ____

Bonus Box: On the back of this sheet, write five words that can be used to describe an apple.

©The Mailbox® • Back-to-School • TEC1498 • Key p. 93

83

"A-peel-ing" Punctuation

Read each sentence.
If the sentence has correct punctuation, color the apple.

1. Do you like apples!

2. Boy, I love apples!

3. There are different kinds of apples.

4. Wow, that McIntosh apple is bright red?

5. Are all apples bright red?

6. Golden Delicious apples are golden yellow?

7. Granny Smith apples are bright green.

8. What kind of apple is that dark red apple.

9. That dark red apple is called a Delicious apple.

10. Gee, that small apple is red, yellow, and green!

11. That might be a Jonathan apple?

12. Let's eat an apple right now!

In each apple below, write the number of a sentence with incorrect punctuation.
On the line, rewrite the sentence so that it has correct punctuation.

_____

_____

_____

_____

_____

Bonus Box: On the back of this sheet, list three things people can make with apples.

©The Mailbox® • Back-to-School • TEC1498 • Key p. 93

Who Was John Chapman?

Read the passage.

John Chapman was an American pioneer who planted numerous apple trees. He planted so many apple trees that people began calling him Johnny Appleseed. John traveled through Ohio and Indiana planting apple orchards as American families traveled west. Stories are often told about how John gave apple seeds and saplings to everyone he met. Some people said John wore a cooking pot for a hat, a coffee sack as a shirt, and no shoes! John is remembered for his apple orchards, love of nature, kindness to animals, and willingness to help others.

1. **Think** about the passage. **Write** a good title for the passage.

   _____

2. **Circle** the word that means "many."

3. **Underline** the sentence that tells why John Chapman was called Johnny Appleseed.

4. **List** the states John Chapman traveled through. _____

   _____

5. **Draw** a box around the word that means "young apple trees."

6. **Complete** the sentence below.

   Two things that John Chapman is remembered for are _____

   _____

7. **Look** back in the passage. **Draw** a line through the sentence that does not belong.

8. **Explain** what a *pioneer* is. _____

Bonus Box: List three new or interesting words from the passage.

Nouns Rule!

These cool school tools think nouns rule!
Read what each tool has to say about nouns.
Cut out each word below and glue it on a chart.

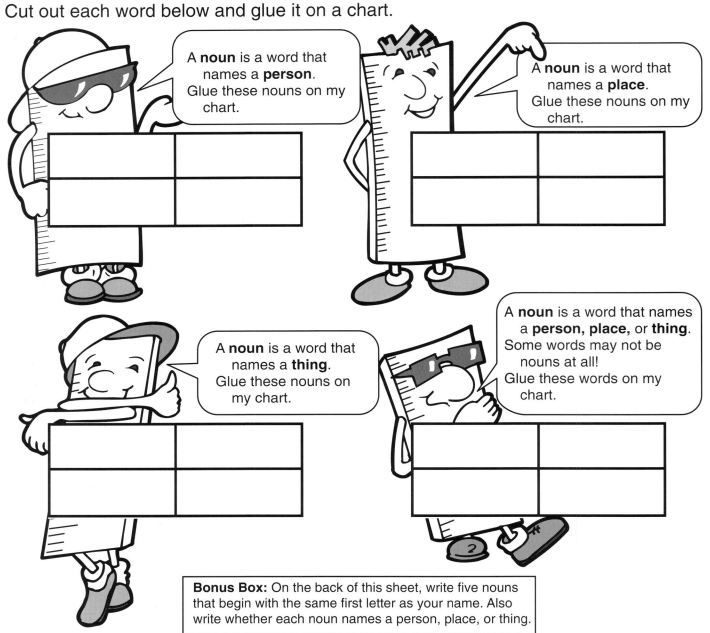

A **noun** is a word that names a **person**. Glue these nouns on my chart.

A **noun** is a word that names a **place**. Glue these nouns on my chart.

A **noun** is a word that names a **thing**. Glue these nouns on my chart.

A **noun** is a word that names a **person, place,** or **thing**. Some words may not be nouns at all! Glue these words on my chart.

Bonus Box: On the back of this sheet, write five nouns that begin with the same first letter as your name. Also write whether each noun names a person, place, or thing.

©The Mailbox® • *Back-to-School* • TEC1498 • Key p. 94

teacher	book	playground	chalk
read	classroom	learn	principal
scissors	listen	secretary	share
paper	office	student	cafeteria

Name _____

Proper Noun Pursuit

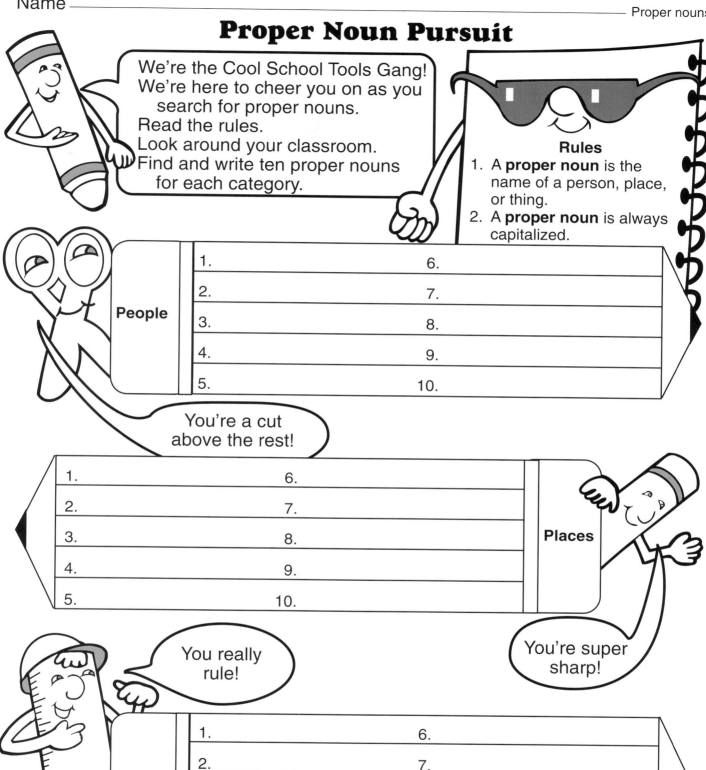

We're the Cool School Tools Gang!
We're here to cheer you on as you search for proper nouns.
Read the rules.
Look around your classroom.
Find and write ten proper nouns for each category.

Rules
1. A **proper noun** is the name of a person, place, or thing.
2. A **proper noun** is always capitalized.

People
1.	6.
2.	7.
3.	8.
4.	9.
5.	10.

You're a cut above the rest!

Places
1.	6.
2.	7.
3.	8.
4.	9.
5.	10.

You really rule!

You're super sharp!

Things
1.	6.
2.	7.
3.	8.
4.	9.
5.	10.

Bonus Box: On the back of this sheet, draw three new members of the Cool School Tools Gang. Use proper nouns to give each member a first and a last name.

Noteworthy Nouns

Read each noun on the word list.
Check the box if the noun is plural.
Follow the rules to change each singular noun to a plural noun.
Then write the plural noun on a blank beside the correct rule.

Word List

☐ address
☐ bench
☐ books
☐ bus
☐ candies
☐ clock
☐ copies
☐ crayons
☐ desk
☐ dictionary
☐ globe
☐ hobby
☐ indexes
☐ journals
☐ library
☐ lunchbox
☐ rulers
☐ shelves
☐ story
☐ weekday

s

_____
_____
_____
_____

Rule
Most nouns
become plural
when you add *s.*

es

_____
_____
_____
_____

Rule
If a noun ends in *s,*
x, ch, or *sh,* add *es*
to make it plural.

ies

Rule
If a noun ends in
a *consonant* and
y, change the *y* to
an *i* and add *es*
to make it plural.

_____
_____
_____

You've got it dude!
Thumbs up to
plural nouns!

Bonus Box: Write one plural noun for each letter of the alphabet.

Ordering numbers less than 100

Back-to-School Boogie

Look at the numbers in each set.
Write the numbers in order from least to greatest.

B. 34   40   45   42   38

_____

A. 20   22   31   26   36

_____

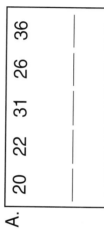

83   80   72   88   75

_____

J. 68   60   72   70   61

_____

E.

D. 12   11   16   13   10

_____

G. 47   40   45   49   51

_____

C. 54   62   52   57   61

_____

F. 43   51   48   52   45

_____

I. 77   89   73   86   72

_____

H. 99   94   85   97   86

_____

Bonus Box: Color the box with the lowest number red. Color the box with the highest number blue.

©The Mailbox® • *Back-to-School* • TEC1498 • Key p. 95

89

Johnny's Apple Orchard

For each tree, study the numbers on the apples.
Find two apples whose difference is equal to the number on
the tree trunk.
Color the two apples red.

Bonus Box: Look at the number on each apple you **did not** color. If the number is odd, color the apple green.

Addition: no regrouping

Hopping Off to School

Which route will these frogs take to school?
To find out, solve each problem.
Then connect each answer less than 50.

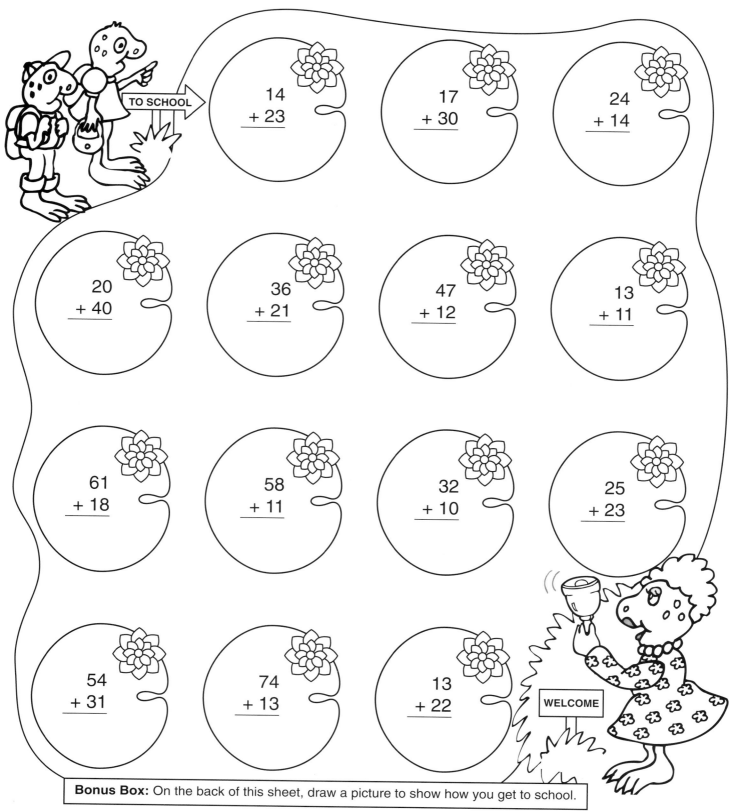

14
+ 23

17
+ 30

24
+ 14

20
+ 40

36
+ 21

47
+ 12

13
+ 11

61
+ 18

58
+ 11

32
+ 10

25
+ 23

54
+ 31

74
+ 13

13
+ 22

TO SCHOOL

WELCOME

Bonus Box: On the back of this sheet, draw a picture to show how you get to school.

Planning for a Great Year

Help Ms. Leaper plan how to organize her students.
Color and cut out Ms. Leaper's students below.
Use the students to help you solve each problem.
Write your answers on the lines.

A. How many boys and girls are there in Ms. Leaper's class? _____	B. If 6 boys and 3 girls bring lunch to school, how many lunches does Ms. Leaper need to order from the cafeteria? _____	C. If Ms. Leaper puts students in pairs for reading, how many pairs will there be? _____
D. If girls only pair with girls, how many pairs of girls will there be? _____	E. If boys only pair with boys, how many pairs of boys will there be? _____	F. If Ms. Leaper sends 4 pairs of students to the media center, how many pairs will still be in the classroom? _____
G. If Ms. Leaper puts 4 students in each math group, how many groups will there be? _____	H. If Ms. Leaper makes 4 equal science groups, how many students will be in each group? _____	I. If Ms. Leaper makes 2 social studies groups of 7 students, how many students will be left for the third group? _____

Bonus Box: How many students are in your classroom? Write your answer on the back of this sheet.

Answer Keys

Page 44
1. reading
2. math
3. art
4. spelling
5. writing
6. social studies
7. science
8. music

Page 83

1. . (red)
2. ? (green)
3. . (red)
4. ? (green)
5. . (red)
6. . (red)
7. ? (green)
8. . (red)
9. ? (green)
10. . (red)
11. . (red)
12. . (red)

Order of answers below may vary.

| 1 | 3 | 5 | 6 |
| 8 | 10 | 11 | 12 |

Bonus Box: Answers may vary. Possible answers include the following: *shiny, small, smooth, round,* and *red.*

Page 84

1. Do you like apples!
2. Boy, I love apples!
3. There are different kinds of apples.
4. Wow, that McIntosh apple is bright red?
5. Are all apples bright red?
6. Golden Delicious apples are golden yellow?
7. Granny Smith apples are bright green.
8. What kind of apple is that dark red apple.
9. That dark red apple is called a Delicious apple.
10. Gee, that small apple is red, yellow, and green!
11. That might be a Jonathan apple?
12. Let's eat an apple right now!

In each apple below, write the number of a sentence with incorrect punctuation. On the line, rewrite the sentence so that it has correct punctuation.

1. Do you like apples?
4. Wow, that McIntosh apple is bright red!
6. Golden Delicious apples are golden yellow.
8. What kind of apple is that dark red apple?
11. That might be a Jonathan apple.

Bonus Box: Answers will vary.

Page 85

1. Answers will vary. Accept reasonable responses.
2. numerous
3. He planted so many apple trees that people began calling him Johnny Appleseed.
4. Ohio, Indiana
5. saplings
6. Accept any two of the following: apple orchards, love of nature, kindness to animals, willingness to help others.
7. Some people said John wore a cooking pot for a hat, a coffee sack as a shirt, and no shoes!
8. A pioneer is an early settler.

Bonus Box: Answers will vary.

Page 86

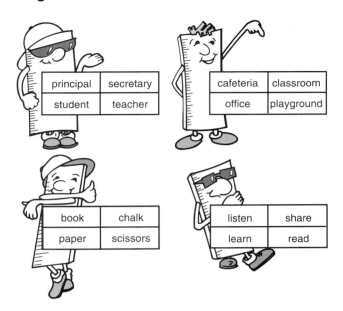

| principal | secretary |
| student | teacher |

| cafeteria | classroom |
| office | playground |

| book | chalk |
| paper | scissors |

| listen | share |
| learn | read |

Bonus Box: Answers will vary.

Page 88

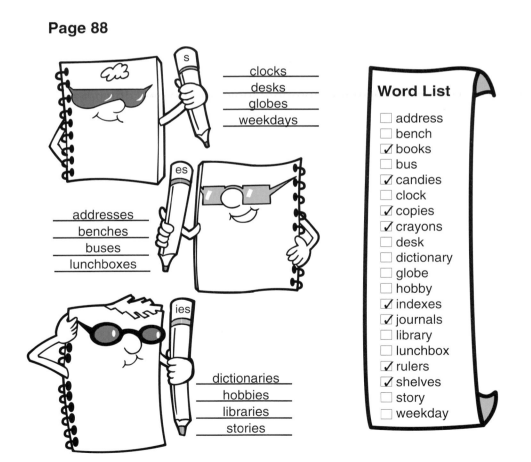

clocks
desks
globes
weekdays

addresses
benches
buses
lunchboxes

dictionaries
hobbies
libraries
stories

Word List

☐ address
☐ bench
☑ books
☐ bus
☑ candies
☐ clock
☑ copies
☑ crayons
☐ desk
☐ dictionary
☐ globe
☐ hobby
☑ indexes
☑ journals
☐ library
☐ lunchbox
☑ rulers
☑ shelves
☐ story
☐ weekday

Bonus Box: Answers will vary.

Page 89

A.	20	22	26	31	36
B.	34	38	40	42	45
C.	52	54	57	61	62
D.	10	11	12	13	16
E.	72	75	80	83	88
F.	43	45	48	51	52
G.	40	45	47	49	51
H.	85	86	94	97	99
I.	72	73	77	86	89
J.	60	61	68	70	72

Bonus Box: Students should have colored box D red and box H blue.

Page 90

The apples with the numbers indicated below should be colored red.

A. 17 and 9
B. 11 and 6
C. 1 and 0
D. 11 and 8
E. 9 and 2
F. 18 and 9
G. 11 and 3
H. 10 and 4
I. 12 and 8
J. 9 and 7

Bonus Box: The apples with the numbers indicated below should be colored green.

A. 15
B. 1 and 7
C. 9, 7, and 3
D. 1 and 7
E. 1
F. 5
G. 5 and 7
H. 7
I. 1 and 3
J. 1, 1, and 13

Page 91

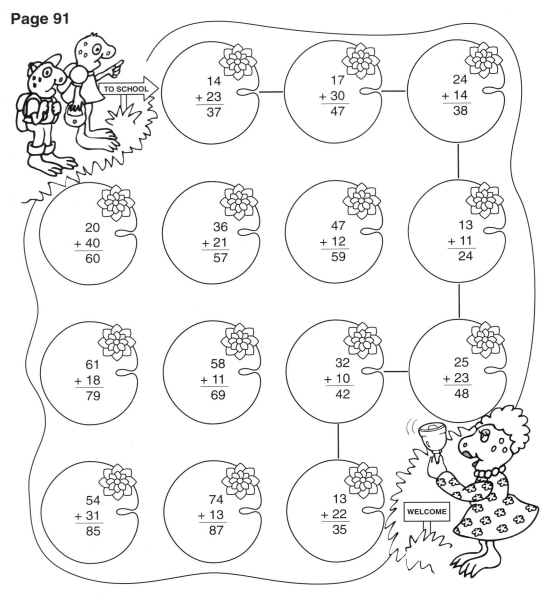

TO SCHOOL

$$\begin{array}{r} 14 \\ + 23 \\ \hline 37 \end{array}$$

$$\begin{array}{r} 17 \\ + 30 \\ \hline 47 \end{array}$$

$$\begin{array}{r} 24 \\ + 14 \\ \hline 38 \end{array}$$

$$\begin{array}{r} 20 \\ + 40 \\ \hline 60 \end{array}$$

$$\begin{array}{r} 36 \\ + 21 \\ \hline 57 \end{array}$$

$$\begin{array}{r} 47 \\ + 12 \\ \hline 59 \end{array}$$

$$\begin{array}{r} 13 \\ + 11 \\ \hline 24 \end{array}$$

$$\begin{array}{r} 61 \\ + 18 \\ \hline 79 \end{array}$$

$$\begin{array}{r} 58 \\ + 11 \\ \hline 69 \end{array}$$

$$\begin{array}{r} 32 \\ + 10 \\ \hline 42 \end{array}$$

$$\begin{array}{r} 25 \\ + 23 \\ \hline 48 \end{array}$$

$$\begin{array}{r} 54 \\ + 31 \\ \hline 85 \end{array}$$

$$\begin{array}{r} 74 \\ + 13 \\ \hline 87 \end{array}$$

$$\begin{array}{r} 13 \\ + 22 \\ \hline 35 \end{array}$$

WELCOME

Bonus Box: Drawings will vary.

Page 92

A. 20
B. 11
C. 10
D. 4
E. 6
F. 6
G. 5
H. 5
I. 6

Bonus Box: Answers should correctly tell how many students are in your class.